WHATEVER HAPPENED TO THE
Sunday School
CLASS OF '66

WHATEVER HAPPENED TO THE
Sunday School
CLASS OF '66

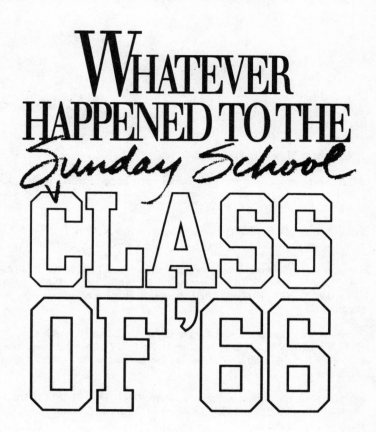

Paula Rinehart

THOMAS NELSON PUBLISHERS
Nashville

Copyright © 1991 by Paula Rinehart

Published in Nashville, Tennessee, by Thomas Nelson, Inc., and distributed in Canada by Lawson Falle, Ltd., Cambridge, Ontario.

Scripture quotations noted NASB are taken from THE NEW AMERICAN STANDARD BIBLE. Copyright © 1960, 1962, 1963, 1968, 1971, 1973, 1975, 1977 by The Lockman Foundation and are used by permission.

Scripture quotations marked NIV are taken from The Holy Bible: NEW INTERNATIONAL VERSION. Copyright © 1978 by the New York International Bible Society. Used by permission of Zondervan Bible Publishers.

Scripture quotations are from the NEW KING JAMES VERSION of the Bible. Copyright © 1979, 1980, 1982, Thomas Nelson, Inc., Publishers.

Poem excerpt on 202 reprinted from "Act III, Scene ii" in *The Weather of the Heart* by Madeleine L'Engle © 1978 by Crosswicks. Used by permission of Harold Shaw Publishers, Wheaton, IL.

Library of Congress Cataloging-in-Publication Data
Rinehart, Paula.
    Whatever happened to the Sunday school class of '66 / Paula Rinehart.
        p.   cm.
    ISBN 0-8407-7644-6 (hard)
    1. Middle aged persons—Religious life. 2. Middle age. 3. Rinehart, Paula. I. Title.
    BV4579.5.R55 1991
    248.8'4—dc20   91-18303
                                                              CIP

Printed in the United States of America

20009   1 2 3 4 5 6 7 - 96 95 94 93 92 91

Contents

      Moving Beyond the Simple Answers   171
12 *Saving the World*
      What Happened When We Didn't   189
13 *Fresh Starts*
      Embracing a Realistic Hope   203

      Notes   217

      About the Author   221

"Behold, I lay in Zion a choice stone,
a precious cornerstone,
And he who believes in Him
shall not be disappointed."

1 Peter 2:6 (NASB)

To Stacy
who shared this book with me

Preface

When I began this book, I could not even begin to envision the note on which it would end. More accurately, I was afraid of the note on which it would end.

I realized that during many of the months spent writing I was in a tunnel some would call midlife. Only I had no assurance that it was possible to come out on the other side—renewed and better for all the wear. All I could see then was a kind of disillusionment that threatened to leave me jaded, and for all I knew at the time, maybe greys and browns and blacks were all that one could hope for to paint the second half of life. Maybe from here on out you just grunted your way to the grave.

In the midst of it all, I had some of the wild, crazy urges for which midlife is infamous. I thought about learning to hang glide or scuba dive, but my children said they wanted to grow up with their first mother. I counted at least three cosmetic surgeries by which I could profit, though doctors' offices leave me cold. In the end, it seemed better to just face head-on the issues in front of me.

When, after many ups and downs, and ins and outs, I began to sense myself emerging from that dark tunnel, once again seeing the world in living color, I could not have been more surprised. *To what do I attribute this new turn in the road?* I wondered. *Some change of diet? A recent trip overseas? A special act of grace?*

I finally realized it was the actual process of writing on this topic that was bringing about my inner metamorphosis; for as I wrote, I spent hours skimming the cream of nearly fifty conversations with men and women at similar places in their own lives. Little threads of their stories and experiences encouraged me. Their lives mirrored back to me feelings and conclusions that were mine as well. *I've felt that way, too. I just never had a word for it,* was my inner response over and over. For their stories —and in many cases, for their friendships—I owe them more than I can say.

To list all their names would be difficult, but I want to mention a few. To Tony and Becky Metcalf, Marnie Haden, and Maureen Rank: I am grateful for your willingness to let me share in a wide range of your experiences and insights. To Melissa Hammock, Paul Borthwick, Karen D'Arrezzo, Russ Johnston, Brent Curtis, Marty Russell, Ralph Ennis, Bill Barnett, Dave Mayfield, Mike Bellah, Meredith Gandy, Alice Lawhead, Walter Byrd, Jim Duncan, Traci Mullins, Bob Nielson, and Billy Grammar: A special thanks as well for your stories and the candid, refreshing way you opened your lives.

I have often felt overwhelmed by the task of trying to write a perspective that reflects some aspect of a whole generation of people. Undoubtedly, others see our journey differently. Writing on a topic like this is like being a referee in a high school football game, I think—you can only call the play from your particular vantage point.

Nevertheless, I want to acknowledge the help of others who have stood at different points on the field than I and who have shared with me their viewpoints. I am particularly thankful to Jim Dethmer, Dr. John Hannah, George Barna, Jack Skeen, Dr. Jim Engel, Jack Simms, Dan Hays, Dan Allender, William Willemon, Josh McDowell, Dr. J. P. Moreland, Roger Randall, and Fran Sciacca. I am also grateful to Sue Monk Kidd and Calvin Miller, two individuals with special sensitivity and perceptiveness in the arena of life passages.

In this same regard, I would be remiss if I did not acknowledge others who have written more extensively about life stages. The works of Daniel Levinson, Gail

Sheehy, Cheryl Merser, and William Bridges, in particular, have influenced my understanding.

Throughout this book, I have purposefully omitted the names of individuals except for the three whose stories are followed in more detail, lest the reader lose track of who said what and whose story is whose. The true names of these three individuals have been changed, but they represent real and living people, with some details altered to preserve their anonymity. I have spent so much time trafficking through their lives these last two years that they feel like family. My respect and admiration only grows for the way they have confronted their own struggles and disappointments.

It is for all these reasons that writing this book has been a gift to me. My experience has been enriched by the people I have known, by friends who have shared their lives with me. This book brought me around to a deep, genuine sense of gratitude that wells up in me as strongly as the disillusionment ever did.

It is a God-given place, one where I can catch my breath. I stand here encouraged, less aware of what I've lost because I realize there is just so much I've been given in the process.

Paula Rinehart
Raleigh, North Carolina

Part I

The Genesis
of
Big Dreams

CHAPTER 1

An Invitation

I wanted to do something no one had ever done before. I wanted my life to be extraordinary.

Jim Roberts, 45

---◆---

There was a moment, one in particular, when I first *felt* older-than-young. The evidence that I was getting older had been plain enough, to be sure. I could look in the mirror and point out a few gray hairs, and I knew from the growing assortment of moisturizing creams, wrinkle concealers, and styling gels it was taking more time and trouble to look good these days. But I still thought of myself as a woman who at least bordered on the category of "young," until the day a man almost my age changed my perception.

Dressed in gym shorts and solid white Nikes, I was jogging at a perfectly respectable pace on the Y's indoor track during lunch hour. In fact, I was moving faster than many in the crowd. But out of the corner of my eye, I could see a man gaining on me, and in a few seconds, he was squeezing past. I stepped aside to give him room. As he slipped by, he lowered his head and said graciously, "Thank you, Ma'am."

"Ma'am," I said to myself. *Of all the nerve!* I fought the urge to run ahead and ask him if he realized that this was the South and *ma'am* is a term of deference reserved for older women—much older women. "Ma'am is for your mother and your maiden aunt," I wanted to say.

Instead, I just watched him from a distance. His hair

was thinning in the same places mine was peppering with gray. He was no spring chicken himself and certainly in no position to call me "ma'am." I thought about getting a closer look when a little voice in my head restrained me. "You're not eighteen anymore," it said. "You're thirty-eight. Maybe it is starting to show."

It struck me at that moment that maybe, just maybe, I had crossed over into the phase of life known as *middle age.*

I am not alone. At least forty million people are presently making their way through a passage known as "midlife." We are part of a famous group of Americans born after World War II, between 1945 and 1964. Over the years, we have been given many labels: War babies, the Pepsi Generation, the Rock Generation, the Me Generation. We have had many names, but the label used most often is *baby boomers.* I shrink from using that phrase, yet that is what we are.

We have been studied and scrutinized, celebrated and lamented, everything but ignored. Ten years ago the editor of *People* magazine, Landon Jones, wrote a landmark biography of our generation called *Great Expectations: America and the Baby Boom Generation.* Because there were so many of us heading into the tumultuous middle years of life, he predicted that our culture would soon be immersed in the throes of midlife on a mass scale.[1]

A few years later, Michael Nichols, director of an outpatient psychiatric clinic, wrote a book entitled *Turning 40 in the '80s.* He confirmed that the large number of "profoundly troubled" thirty-five to forty-five year olds who came in for treatment were struggling with their transition from youth to middle age. The rise of stress and anxiety among those in our generation shows what indicators we are indeed having more difficulty adjusting our dreams to reality. Like time-release capsules all going off at the same time, we are confronting in earnest the issues that make up this notorious passage in life.

Midlife is no picnic for anyone, for any generation. It can be a trying time filled with questions, confusion, and an internal scorecard of losses. A host of ambivalent feelings accompany the questions: *What's missing here? Why can't I finally get what I want? What do I want, anyway?* This is when the ideals of youth crash head-on into some of the hard, immovable barriers of real life. It's no wonder midlife is often the infamous harbinger of anxiety and disappointment.

But there are two reasons why the passage through these years promises to be even more challenging for those of us born in the twenty-year span following World War II. The first relates to our place in this century. The prosperous "good time" decades of the '50s and '60s, when we grew up, led us to expect a lot out of life and, consequently, to a greater downfall later.

We were wonder children, born in wonder years with all the advantages and opportunities our parents could bring our way. Scarcity and hardship—those words belonged to a generation which had grown up through the Great Depression and World War II. Our generation was beyond that. These were the good times, the good life, and we were invited to claim our share. The world was our stage, and we found out too late that not everyone would get to be a star. This was the foundation of our great expectations, one explanation for why we now find life more problem-plagued, more overwhelming than we would have thought.

The second reason relates to the renaissance of interest in Christianity that took place in our age group during the '60s, and much of the '70s. The years 1966–1972 are increasingly regarded as marking a "mini-revival" among youth.[2] The Jesus Movement and the explosion of campus parachurch groups, like Campus Crusade, the Navigators, and Intervarsity, gained tremendous momentum during this period. Josh McDowell, who has spoken on college and high school campuses for more than twenty-five years, said he had never seen equaled the degree of enthusiasm and spiritual interest he saw among youth during those six to ten years.

That spiritual awakening, with its accompanying effervescence and idealism, coincided with our formative years. Authors William Straus and Neil Howe, in their book *Generations: The History of America's Future 1584–2069*, conclude that our generation is one of five in American history that qualify for the label "idealist," generations who also wanted to change the status quo: the Puritans (1584–1614); those of the Great Awakening (1701–1723); the Transcendentalists (1792–1821); and those of the Missionary Alliance (1860–1882).

In our case, our idealism led us to establish unconscious connections between our expectations of life—which were big enough already—and our faith in God. Thus from two avenues, one cultural and the other religious, we have the makings of a more turbulent, disillusioning passage through our middle years than any generation in this century.

SOMETHING FEELS WRONG

The first hints of "something amiss" tend to sneak up on people at different ages and circumstances. For me, the critical birthday was right in the middle of the two most notable ones, age thirty and age forty. Though I concealed my misgivings well, the year I turned thirty-five was pivotal. I felt like the rug had been pulled out from under me, like someone who had been standing on a street corner, waiting for a bus, and now I suddenly realized it was never going to come.

I was face to face with the unwelcome realization that my life showed every evidence of working out much differently than I had pictured. Somewhere in my past, without realizing it, I had forecast a time in the future when I would feel I had finally *arrived.* I would have a career moving full speed ahead, overachieving children, close friends, an attentive husband, a well-decorated home—some litany like that, anyway.

I had never formally laid out all my hopes. I only knew that there was too great a disparity between the kind of life I had dreamed of and the kind of life I had. I felt shaken.

It was not that my life was noticeably unpleasant. I lived in a house on a quiet street with books in every corner and plants in the windows, with a husband and two children, a dog and a station wagon. My life was nothing if not ordinary, and that was much of the problem. It was so ordinary, so middle-aged, so predictable. So disappointing.

The excitement and wonderlust, that take-on-the-world enthusiasm of my earlier days was missing and I didn't know where it had gone. I was left peeking out from behind a stack of bills and unironed shirts. The discovery that life had fallen woefully short of my expectations coincided with another discovery, the kind that only true packrats can appreciate.

I was on a wild chase for a wayward quotation one morning when there in the closet of our study I spotted an old cardboard box. It was the label that got me. I rubbed away a fit of dust and read "College: 1966–1970." Here was one of those cartons my husband had toted in and out of four states because, someday, his wife just might want to rummage through its contents.

Curiosity made me lift the lid and take a peek inside. At first glance I almost gathered the whole of it to cart to the trashcan. But then my hands began to leaf through the worn pages and mementos, and before long, I simply cleared out a spot in the corner of the closet. There I let the memories do their magic.

What struck me first was the scarcity of sorority party

favors and other standard college memorabilia. Instead I thumbed through dog-eared sermon notes and faded blue booklets that communicated the basic message of Christianity in four concise points. Brochures for weekend conferences and snapshots of old friends with our bags packed stared up at me. There were a couple of books on the Second Coming of Christ and a big red notebook of basic youth conflicts that I had felt compelled to save. Truly, the spiritual paraphernalia of another era.

The great find of the morning, though, was my first Bible—the New American Standard Version I had chosen on my own. When I saw that it was still covered in "Blueprint for Revolution" paper, I had to smile. What had become of the young college girl who had eagerly scribbled the notes in its margins?

Slowly, the significance of the contents of this box came clear. These were the markings of the first leg of my own spiritual journey, the transcendent place where I first looked beyond my own life to find an anchor of meaning, purpose, and self-identity. Here, in the contents of this carton, I was looking at part of the genesis of my understanding of life and God and faith, and what I might expect from all three. There was surely some connection between that gnawing sense of personal disappointment and the spiritual dreams that lay shrouded in this box.

I started to pay closer attention.

WHERE DO YOU FIT?

In recent years it has been common, sometimes wearily so, to look back twenty years to an era when the largest generation in U.S. history was in the heyday of its youth. We've seen old film clips of draft card burnings and assassinations, of Lyndon Johnson reading his exit speech and flower children on the streets of San Francisco—all replayed by the same television networks who filmed them in the first place. A strange feeling sets in. The memories are so universal it seems as though you were *there*, when in actuality, most of us saw the big happenings on television—even the first go-round.

Even now, questions come up in some unrelated conversation that show both the one asking and the one answering recognize their similar vintage. "What were *you* doing in the Sixties?" someone asks. Whether or not you went to Vietnam, where you were the day Kennedy was shot, were you into the drug scene in college—small connections in the present are made out of shared memories in the past.

When the question of my whereabouts during that period of time is posed I have to catch myself before the words slip out of my mouth. Sometimes I feel the overwhelming urge to tell the truth: *I was in Sunday school.*

Well, maybe not *literally* Sunday school, but awfully close. A Christian conference, a Bible study group, having coffee and deep conversation with a friend—something spiritual and intense.

Where were you? To what extent do you identify yourself with the larger picture of your generation? Did you have dreams that were fueled by a period of spiritual idealism and enthusiasm? Perhaps you can find yourself in these truth-or consequences questions that help a person distinguish his generational roots.[3]

◆

- Do you remember the *debut* of Barbie and Batman?
- Can you give the names of the Cartwright brothers from the television show *Bonanza?*
- Do you have a sharp mental picture of the dressed-and-pressed image of Beaver and Wally's mother, June?
- Can you remember a few lines from Lovin' Spoonful's *Do You Believe in Magic?* or Simon and Garfunkel's *Sounds of Silence?*

• Do the good ol' days seem more pleasant to you than the ones you're experiencing now?

• Do you ever feel like a victim of your times?

• Are you ever anxious or depressed?

• Do you ever feel like you deserved something you didn't get or got something you didn't deserve?

• Do you remember your youth as a basically happy time with some big dreams that have gone mostly unrealized?

• Have you eaten a Dove Bar?

• Do you ever find yourself trying to make up for the big things you can't have by indulging in the little things you can?

• Have you changed jobs or locations often?

• Are you threatened by long-term intimate relationships?

• Do you use vacations, shopping trips, or videos to cheer yourself up?

• Do you buy too much on credit?

• Do you ever wonder if you're becoming cynical and withdrawn, suspicious of advertising, government policy, and big financial appeals?

• Do you ever feel like, deep down, there's no one but yourself you can trust?

• Were there social and spiritual ideals you embraced at a younger age—like making your life count for something significant or changing society for the better—and now, you sometimes wonder what happened to all of that?

———————————————— ◆ ————————————————

If a good many of these questions brought a "yes" answer from your lips, then feel free to congratulate yourself. You are a product of your times. And if, like me, you hate being stereotyped and lumped into someone else's statistical glob, then take courage. You are merely discovering a few of your basic tendencies and inclinations, which, though rooted in your past, have bearing on your present and your future.

As I've thought about my own life and listened to others, I've discovered that our individual stories, our lives, have been shaped much more than we realize by the times in which we've lived. There are vast numbers of us who began with high hopes and great expectations, who have smarted as those hopes and expectations have been shrunk to a smaller, more life-like size. A great collection of us thought that if we worked hard and believed well, if we followed our dreams, the road would rise to meet us. Adding faith in an all-powerful God to that sequence seemed only to baptize the whole equation. And, as we'll see, it set us up for a tremendous fall.

REAL LIVES, REAL STORIES

Though the facts that surround the journey of our generation are well-chronicled in fancy marketing strategies and predictions for our future, it is *the lives of individuals* that have interested me most. The real story is told in how we have grappled with our original dreams, with our relationships and hopes for change. Growing up and growing older has thrust on us struggles with careers and marriages, uncertainties about our faith and our selves— very little of which we expected to encounter.

Our story cannot be told sufficiently in divorce statistics and income projections. There is another side. Sure, we're less political, less rich, and less trusting than most people expected, but there is much more to telling our story. What have we, as individuals, done with all those big dreams, with our longing to make a difference? Where are we *now* as we meander through midlife?

No one lets go of old dreams or false illusions easily. In this book, I hope to share with you the struggles and hard-won spiritual insights of many people who count themselves among the postwar generation. I purposefully want to concentrate on a few in particular. Out of many possibilities I have chosen four individuals.

The first one, Ted, is a man in his mid-thirties who owns a floral business. He has battled his way through near-bankruptcy in a city in much greater need of new jobs than fresh flowers. His struggle centers around the realization that he may never be able to take off and soar the way he'd hoped. He has learned to taste a measure of success in just hanging in there.

A sharp-looking man with prematurely grey hair, if you were to meet Ted somewhere today, there are two qualities about him that would particularly impress you. The first is his genuineness. In the confusing world of owning your own business, Ted has been quick to face his mistakes and admit his failures. He's not trying to paint a glossy picture of his life that isn't real. The second quality that stands out in Ted is sheer perseverance. He has stuck it out in a difficult situation long after other people would have thrown in the towel. If anyone has deserved to do well, it is Ted.

Susan is, likewise, pushing forty. She works in public relations for a company headquartered in the northwest, where she lives with her two daughters. What Susan had wanted most out of life was an intimate, lasting relationship. Fifteen years ago, though, she married a man she met in college, a man whose spiritual zeal took him on to seminary. There the emotional instability of his background surfaced, leaving Susan to raise two girls alone.

Susan is a woman who has a great deal to give. She is someone who has only recently gained an awareness of herself and a deeper understanding of others. She had believed that what best cured a man's ills was a good woman.

Some of us have reached the goals, the dreams we set out to reach. Such is the case of Grant, a tall, lanky psychiatrist with a booming counseling practice and national recognition. Grant is a good example of the most curious kind of disappointment to be found in our generation. His life is the story of what happens when you get what you thought you wanted, only to discover that it must not be what you wanted after all. Maybe you don't even know what it is you really want. Even fulfilled dreams leave a lot of restlessness and longing for something more.

Grant spends his days with a steady stream of people who need someone to help them sort out the pieces of their tangled lives. He returns home—too late, he says— to a wife and four children who want a father and a husband who has time for them, too. And Grant, where does he get some of the boost that everyone else looks to him for? That's a question he asks himself as he races through his days, sometimes honking at his own tail lights.

And lastly, myself, for a very simple reason. I know that story best. I bring the perspective of a writer whose temperament is cursed with the ability to see what could be and what ought to be, long before I see what *is*.

I grew up in a small town in Virginia with one high school, a town where no one locked their car doors and anyone would take your check. A town so vanilla in entertainment that the lives of its adults centered around the sports programs, budding romances, and wedding showers of their kids. The message that came through loud and clear was, "You're special, we're behind you, you can go out there and knock 'em dead." My children wish we would take them back there to live. I tell them that while I had a great support system, it made for some harsh encounters with the real world later on.

As an adult, or some facsimile thereof, I have lived with the illusion that I could finally get *set* in life. I could sit back and coast because some achievement would have put me over the top. It hasn't. I have been deeply committed to the idea that if you worked hard enough, or trusted God enough, then anything was possible. It isn't. Taking no for an answer is not my style. Facing disappointment and letting go of some of my big dreams has not been easy.

The four of us, as well as the many other individuals whose stories are shared in this book, represent those in our generation who, in some unseen way, attached many of their expectations of life to their concept of trusting God. As these stories unfold, you will be able to observe the process by which a person begins to bring some of their expectations into line with reality. When we face our disappointments head-on it affects our closest relationships, our whole notion of the good life, our appreciation for the role we play in a larger world. We discover that it is possible not only to grow up, but to grow beyond our dreams into a tangible sense of gratitude and a joy in the adventure of living life as we find it.

But first, I have to ask you to indulge yourself a few minutes of regression. In the next chapter you will meet each of these four individuals as college students. I hope to let you take a peak into their lives twenty years ago, to feel some of the optimism and great hopes with which they began. This is a small slice out of the past, one place where some of our expectations fused with our understanding of God. The setting is as it was, a Sunday school class two blocks from a large eastern university.

I invite you to trek along with me, with us, in a personal but generational journey through time. I think you will see how disillusionment can so often lead to something better—a genuine appreciation for the tentative, trusting nature of a life lived with God. Many of us have traded hype and naivete for a taste of a reality that feels pretty good, when all is said and done.

Perhaps you have made this transition. If so, what follows should encourage you to keep pressing on. On the other hand, you may be discouraged or depressed by too many dreams dying before your eyes. In that case, I hope this book opens for you a new vista, a new way of seeing as you move into the future.

Regardless of your circumstances, if you're of my generation, you will likely be able to hear your own voice spoken here through someone else's; and in their stories, I think you will find a measure of your own.

CHAPTER 2

Whatever Happened to the Sunday School Class of '66?

The years 1966–1972 were some of my favorites. The atmosphere on college campuses was absolutely electric.

Josh McDowell, Campus speaker

---✦---

The morning sun was simply too warm for the end of May and the room, already packed with college kids, seemed to bulge like an overstuffed suitcase.

The longer I sat in my folding chair, the more inviting a spot standing in the back became. There by the door at least the air stirred. Whoever decided that women should appear in church in dresses and hose had probably never worn either, I thought.

I gave up my folding chair to an eager soul less bothered by the heat and assumed a place by the wall—a decision easily made since, by now, there were only a few places left anywhere. It was almost time for the class to begin. The old Presbyterian fellowship hall, only a few blocks from campus, had become a Christian gathering place for college students. Everyone knew, in this my freshman year, the spring of 1966, that if you wanted a seat you had to come early.

What a collage of students came through those doors every week. A fair number looked as though they had been born in a church pew, their Bibles sliding automatically into invisible slots beneath their elbows. But more and more, it was the sheer variety that made the group exciting. Where else did a campus jock mix any easier with guys whose long hair formed the most obvious ring around their collars?

Between the rattle of folding chairs and a faint low hum of conversation, this class was never what you might call quiet. Even the teacher practiced a kind of voice projection that added a few decibels to the microphone. The trouble was, too many of us knew each other.

Whether from small group Bible studies or summer beach projects, our paths had crossed somewhere in the underground network of parachurch groups that dotted the college scene. That was part of the charm. You felt, and rightly so, that you were part of something much larger than yourself.

We were all waiting for the main attraction and he did not disappoint us. The class was taught by a young lawyer; a sharp, articulate man in his early thirties who applied the same relentless scrutiny to Romans on Sunday morning that he did to his court case on Monday.

He always began with a few old Johnny Carson jokes that seemed out of character for him, and that's what made them funny. Then without warning he would shift gears.

"Turn in your Bibles," Frank was saying now, "to the first chapter of Romans. Read the last two paragraphs closely and tell me, what explanation do you see in those verses for how a culture, a society becomes corrupt?"

All over the room you could hear the soft crackle of pages being turned, the sound ricocheting off the checkered linoleum floor. Then silence—or something as close to silence as this room ever got.

Frank had the ability to pull the whole group along with him in a kind of mental, spiritual jaunt that in the end made you huff and puff like you'd been climbing steep hills all morning. He made you think. You left his class feeling the force of the words, the radical nature of the message. God was who he said he was in the Bible.

He created the world and set apart a small group of people called the Israelites, through whom he revealed even more of his character and power. He was the one who altered history by becoming flesh and blood for a season of thirty-three years, the one who would eventually sum up all of history in his son, Jesus. God was not someone to be messed with casually.

What Frank modeled was a reality I did not come to college believing was possible. He was a *thinking Christian,* a description I considered a contradiction in terms. It still amazed me that you could combine faith and intelligence in the same package.

Growing up in a small town in Thomas Jefferson's Virginia had left its mark on me. There, religion had its place—one that was quiet, unassuming and carefully confined to Sunday morning. It seemed that the green canopy of oak and dogwood trees we lived beneath formed a protective shelter against a more menacing world. In this southern town, life was as uncomplicated as a recipe for sweet potato pie. You knew better than to wear jeans to the grocery store; table cloths ought never to hang more than six inches over the edge; and men, not women, took out the trash. Here in the mid-1960s the rules were still clear.

The only problem in this tidy scheme was that somewhere there were American boys, not resting in the same shade, but slogging their way through the steamy jungles of Vietnam. One young man from our community had already died there. His father's only son, he had been in Vietnam less than a week when he stepped on the land mine that took his life. It was the dark cloud of Vietnam that gave an ominous quality to everything. During the past year American troops had gone from an advisory to an offensive role. The casualties were mounting.

The nightly news shifted its focus like the spotlight on a three-ring circus. One moment you were watching war protestors with angry faces and signs that read, "Who are we to police the world?" Then suddenly the screen would flash the heavily-jowled face of Lyndon Johnson, in deep Texas drawl, promising his "Great Society." Set against the backdrop of race riots in Watts and Atlanta, such a promise seemed like a fairy tale set in another millennium.

These were the rumblings that stirred me out of my nest of false security. Suddenly, going away to college seemed like the right time to ask more cosmic questions. I mean, after figuring out how to get all your classes on Monday, Wednesday and Friday, could someone please explain the meaning of life? Was it possible, even, to make sense of an existence that could be vaporized in an instant to little more than a puff of smoke? Such questions provided the gateway to my first solid understanding of the Christian faith, and I entered with all the enthusiasm of one who felt she had discovered a brave, new world.

Now, standing in the back of this Sunday school class, I shifted my stance to spare my feet. I was amazed at how many heads I recognized. People-watching being among my favorite pastimes, I rather enjoyed looking out over this crowd.

I found one couple near the front particularly interesting. Jim had driven three hundred miles to spend the weekend with Susan. Judging from the way they looked now, it had been a good weekend. I suspected there would be wedding plans in the works before long.

Even in this large crowd you could pick them out as a couple, not two singles who happened to occupy adjacent seats. They were together. Susan seemed especially pleased, sporting the smile of a contented woman.

I had been in the Bible study Susan led in my dorm, and over the course of the year we had become friends. With deep-set brown eyes and thick curly hair that bounced when she laughed, Susan was a wonderful mix of faith and adventure. She could think up some of the wildest ideas—like the time she disguised dog food as a barbecue sandwich and fed it to a friend who ate the whole thing. He might have never been the wiser except that Susan could not resist the temptation to ad lib a dog bark when he finished.

In more sedate confines, like a small group Bible study, her adventurous spirit translated into one of confidence —not the cocky kind, but one that simply believed God could be counted on. I liked that, and I liked her.

Many of us had been following Susan and Jim's romance this year with growing interest. They had met the previous summer at a ten-week Christian training program known as a "beach project," where students converged on a vacation spot and learned how to share their faith by talking to those who would listen. Since that time, Susan and Jim had been in debt to the phone company in an effort to continue their relationship. Occasionally they spent a rare weekend in the same location, but for the most part their relationship had been long distance.

It was a relationship we all rather envied. You could not ask for a more considerate, attentive guy than Jim. His father was a successful lawyer who had greater ambitions for his bright son, but Jim was determined to go to seminary. His spiritual commitment appeared unshakable. It was that aura of good intentions that seemed to insure Susan and Jim's relationship, to give it a glow that others lacked.

If Susan had any doubts that God was leading the two of them together, she didn't voice them. I asked her once how she could be so sure. She thought for a moment. "I think it's mainly the way I feel when I pray with him," she replied. "I just really respect his walk with God."

And what did she think about the possibility of becoming a pastor's wife? That's where her face drew one of the few blanks I could ever remember. "Well, I guess that will be all right, too," she said.

This class was normally a bit more lively than it seemed this morning. But then, I realized, I hadn't been as tuned in as I usually was, either.

It's hard to tell who is challenging what when you're sitting down, hemmed in by a sea of surrounding faces. But from my present vantage point, I knew immediately who the bony arm belonged to that had been stuck so patiently in the air for the last minute or so. Finally, Frank let Grant have the floor. Not the least bit shy, Grant always stood to voice his thoughts or ask a question.

"Look," he said, "we all agree that, without God, man can fall to the depths of depravity and despair. I don't have any problem with that. But how do you account for man's achievements—his compassion, his integrity— some of which he often demonstrates while denying that God even exists? What do you do with that?"

Grant had a way of picking up the pace of any discussion. He didn't really mean to throw a wrench into Frank's carefully-wrought argument. He couldn't help it. He was the kind of guy who thought and wrestled on a deeper level than most of us. The way I figured it, Grant had probably been asking "What is the meaning of all this?" questions since he first looked out of his playpen.

For a couple of minutes, everyone just sat there and waited for Frank to respond. But Frank was in no hurry. He never was. Finally, a guy dressed in a plaid suit that was one size too small jumped into the awkward silence.

"Well, I don't know if you could call man's achievements *real* achievements, if he insists on ignoring God," he said with a note of premature finality. I saw a couple of heads nod in agreement as though that settled that. But one look at Frank's face told me otherwise.

"Wait a minute. It's not that simple," the girl beside Grant ventured rather lamely. Frank urged her on.

"Explain what you mean," he said. "Why isn't it that simple?"

"Well, doesn't it all go back to the beginning, to the fact that man is created in the image of God and capable of greatness?" she said. "Isn't man great but lost?"

As soon as I heard that phrase "great but lost" I knew I was listening to someone who had been reading one of Francis Schaeffer's books. Books of his like *The God Who Is There* and *Escape from Reason* were widely read and discussed. I had a couple of his books on my own shelves.

What was in the air, I wondered, that made life and God and culture so deep and ponderable? Had our parents wrestled this hard to discern the nature of man? Had they even cared? Everywhere these days, someone seemed to be asking Alfie what it was all about and if it was just for the moment they lived.

Apparently, Frank now had an answer he could build on. "Turn back to Genesis," he told the class. "Let's look at what she's saying and see where that greatness comes from."

I stole a look at Grant. He seemed satisfied. Most probably, he had known the answer to what he was asking anyway. He often threw out questions to stimulate the discussion.

Grant was our resident intellectual, a sensitive premed student with an infectious smile and glasses that were Benjamin Franklin round. His build was slight though his limbs were long and gangly, and had I not known him well, I would have thought him a bit of a nerd. What drew me was his intense interest in people, his perception of the places they hurt and the reasons why.

An hour in the student union with him draped over a cup of coffee was an experience all its own. You could be sitting there casually discussing some professor or test when, before you knew it, the conversation invaded your personal space.

Grant would say something like, "This exam seems to

be awfully important to you, Paula. Why is that? What do you think will happen to you if you don't do well?"

"Oh, come on, Grant," I would throw back at him. "Don't you care how well you do? You're the one who has to get into medical school, not me."

"Yeah, I care. I do. But this test seems to be more life-and-deathish to you. I'm just wondering why."

To which we would both just shake our heads and move on, and days later I would find myself asking the same question. Why were grades such a big deal? I hadn't a clue.

Actually, most everything in the spring of '66 was bloated with intensity. The Beatles had recently invaded the United States. Betty Friedan and Ralph Nader were at their zenith. Martin Luther King, Jr. was turning more than a hundred years of black history in the south upside down. And the U.S. was thick into the race to put a man on the moon. Obviously, these were not ordinary times.

I nudged myself back into the present. Somewhere during my daydream, Frank had turned the class over to Ted, who was right in the middle of announcing something that seemed important.

Ted was known to be a great organizer. I was sure he could sell snow to the Eskimos. But whatever Ted was recruiting for this time had galvanized even more of his enthusiasm than usual.

"Look," Ted was saying, "Josh McDowell will be on our campus for four days in just a couple of weeks. Mark the dates on your calendar and bring your friends. He's speaking on sex and the Resurrection and I can't remember the third one, but we expect standing room only. Plan to be there early."

Having said his piece, Ted sat down. That he had become the advance man for Josh McDowell was kind of ironic, I thought.

At one time, Ted had been the social chairman for the Phi Delt house, a proper title for The Party Man. Most of the events he organized then had a couple of kegs in the center of the room. But when a Christian campus group asked him for a night to speak to his house on the relevance of Christianity, Ted was put in a tight spot. How could he say no? Then again, how could he prepare these people for a bunch of guys who had no intention of ever making religion "relevant."

So Ted had let the speakers come. He rounded up a respectable number of brothers and made them promise to be, if not exactly interested, at least polite. Unfortunately—or fortunately, depending on your perspective—Ted listened more than he planned to that night. In a weak moment, he even promised to meet the speaker for coffee in a few days, just to talk.

Somewhere in between, Ted crossed the invisible line in his own spiritual commitment and now, a couple of years later, he had been instrumental in leading a number of his fraternity brothers into a true sense of spiritual brotherhood.

Ted's story is not an unusual one. Sometimes I wondered if someone had put a spiritual potion in the supply of drinking water. People thought a lot—about death and spiritual fulfillment and transfiguration, and they wanted answers that weren't just blowing in the wind.

When I surveyed the crowd of college students who packed this room, I had to conclude that Christianity had greatly benefited from the spiritual urgency of the day. The world did indeed appear reachable for Christ. A hypothesis often shared these days, "the theory of multiplication," was a mathematician's plan demonstrating how it was possible to reach the whole world with the gospel in twenty to forty years. One person would share the gospel with two people who would each tell two more, and from there the numbers would grow exponentially until the task of evangelizing the world was complete. How did the song go? "It only takes a spark to get a fire going. . . ." When I looked out over this crowd, I saw a sea of possible sparks.

Of course, if one got technical, it was possible that some of those "sparks" might not tell another blessed soul. But that didn't seem likely and besides, the suggestion bordered on a lack of faith. Anything seemed possible these days, especially if that something appeared to rest on a spiritual premise.

Now that Frank had finished praying we were free to leave. The fresh air outside was a welcome relief, though no one seemed in much of a rush to go home. We were, in the final analysis, friends—friends who had plans to make and a lot of catching up to do.

There was something else I needed to catch, though, and that was a ride back to my dorm. Who wanted to walk in heels and hose on a day like this? Gratefully, I spotted Jim and Susan on the way to their car. "Have you got room for one more?" I called.

They nodded their answer and smiled at me, at each other.

I ran for the car, and in spite of the hot noon sun, I felt suddenly light, buoyant, and incurably optimistic.

CHAPTER 3

Less Than We Bargained For

The Postwar Generation Grows Up

It's funny, when the Olympics were on last year, I preferred to see them by myself. I cried through every single event —track, swimming, gymnastics. I just wish I could become one of them. I wish I could have been a phenomenon.

Jane Pasturlak, 33

W hat happened?

Bright faces, promising futures. It seemed we had the world almost within our grasp. There were no immovable obstacles in our path—none that couldn't be overcome, anyway. Like newly chosen people, we sat under the blessing of God, protected, hopefully, against real hurt, loss, and failure.

Now, twenty-five years later, if we gather together a similar group, we get a different picture. The jeans are tighter, the bodies inside them have gone south, and there are hairline wrinkles on our faces that no amount of makeup can camouflage. Mortgages and teenagers and briefcases full of paper work have weighted down the old bounce in our steps. "Underneath all my busyness," says one mother and accountant in her thirties, "I find I am mostly just very tired, and a bit bewildered with my life." Gone are the bell bottoms and the catchy religious jargon of our youth. The world around us is still waiting to be changed. Getting the world inside our own four walls under control has proven to be quite a challenge in itself.

The '60s gave way to the individualistic '70s and the greedy '80s. Somewhere in all the froth and foment, easy notions of marriage and family, job security and personal ambitions, and where God fit in the whole picture were severely shaken. The illusion of having it all—well-oiled careers, enough money, quality time with the children, the opportunity to travel—seems more of a myth all the time. Many of us are still playing an internal game of musical chairs, still scrambling to find the Right Job. The sheer force of our numbers has caused job openings to become scarce and a bottleneck at the middle-management level. Career plans have plateaued or stalled in mid-flight, sometimes just when we were within range of our goal.

The acronym that best fits most people our age is one coined by Ron Katz, MOSS: middle-aged, overstressed, semi-affluent, suburbanite. Katz says that the average person in our age group is 41 years old, more overstressed than overworked, and affluent in the loosest sense of the word. We have watched our take-home earnings steadily decline for almost twenty years, while the average price of the most sought-after prize in the American Dream, your own home, has risen to a little more than $100,000.

Coupled with economic strain is the added pressure that comes from breakdown in the family. Our generation is generally credited with the skyrocketing divorce rate, which has ushered in an array of blended families, step-families, and single-parent homes.

We are frequently referred to as "the sandwich generation," caught between competing demands and desires. Our children need parenting, our aging parents need time and attention, and our jobs require more effort for the same income. We are torn between trumped-up ideals we're no longer sure we trust and the longing for a vision to get excited about again. We still want our lives to make a difference, to leave behind more than a marble grave marker with two simple dates. Without a doubt, most of us face our middle years with a sense of how complicated and unpredictable life can turn out to be, and with ample cause for anxiety and stress.

Indeed, the years have sneaked up on us, and, though they have been kinder to some than others, they have gone quickly. Doesn't it seem like yesterday that you were listening to "California Dreaming" while you relaxed, carefree, and dug your toes into warm summer sand? Now you have to turn up the radio to hear it over the din of the kid's carpool on the "Only Oldies" station. It has been a short jaunt from the person you were to the person you are, between the dreams and hopes of then and the present reality of now.

The realization that we are no longer all that young seems to strike people, like it did me, at odd, unguarded moments. One woman claimed that she first felt her age when she took her daughter to a *New Kids on the Block* concert and realized that the only people in the audience who were sitting down were parents her age. "We would meet in the restroom," she explained, "and ask each other what on earth were we doing here. Didn't we walk out of a Rolling Stones concert just yesterday?"

Dave Barry, the humor columnist who wrote a book about the perils of turning forty, says, "I've been hanging around with people roughly my own age for the bulk of my life, and I frankly do not feel that, as a group, we have acquired the wisdom and maturity needed to run the world, or even necessarily power tools."[1] He's convinced that many of us only *look* like grown-ups.

A southern homemaker and mother of three admits that when she looks in the mirror she sees someone who looks as old as she remembers her mother looking when she was a child. Sometimes the image startles her because she says that on the inside, she doesn't "feel that grown-up yet." That's not an uncommon response. Cheryl Merser, in her book about life passages of the postwar generation, writes that though we have indeed grown-up, "we still feel somehow that real adults are in a different category: more certain of their place in the world, wiser, their lives intact in ways we do not yet understand."[2] She says that we are grown-ups still in search of that inner sense of being fully adult.

LOOKING MORE TOGETHER THAN WE FEEL

So while we've managed to live longer in adolescence than any generation preceding us, we have indeed gotten older. There are a few notable characteristics that reflect our lives now, twenty-five years after that youthful era of big dreams and great expectations.

For one thing, the evidence suggests that we have a highly developed ability to look more together than we feel. We know what it takes to make a good impression, how to dress for success, all the right words to say. We have acquired many of the props of middle age—things like insurance policies and riding lawn mowers—that make life feel easier and more secure. But underneath our polished appearances, the anxiety and confusion suggests a very different story.

We are the first generation to make happiness a goal, and yet it is our numbers that have swelled the statistics of depression and suicide. We have virtually created the psychotherapy industry, the number of psychiatrists and psychiatric social workers having tripled since we came along. The recent explosion in small group therapy and study groups reflects our driving need to find a listening ear, someone who can offer insight and understanding about the complexities of our lives. There is much more happening on the inside than our efficient, congenial demeanor would suggest. We often appear to be doing better than we actually are.

A professional woman of thirty-eight who keeps a

busy schedule admits that she often finds herself study-
ing her contemporaries from a distance, wondering if
they share any of her personal misgivings. She wonders if
they ever let mildew grow like mushrooms in their
shower stalls, or question whether they have the nerve to
go back to school and try an entirely new field. Yet she
knows that with her lap-top computer and designer
clothes, she appears every bit as confident and self-as-
sured as her friends and co-workers. So she turns to ther-
apists and her husband and a small Bible study group for
solace.

Sometimes that fragile world beneath the surface of
our life becomes evident during times when we would
normally expect to be at our peak performance. Grant,
the psychologist, discovered this when he was asked to
present his paper on sexual abuse at a national consor-
tium of mental health professionals. Here was an opportunity that represented the reward for his success, a
chance-of-a-lifetime event. Yet he found himself ambivalent about the prospect of presenting his findings. He
began waking up in the middle of the night wondering if
he could really pull it off. Did he have all the data that
was needed? Were his case studies sufficiently docu-
mented? He knew that, for the most part, these were
unreasonable fears, and it dismayed him to be plagued by
the same anxiety he observed in some of his patients.

This kind of anxiety is peculiar to individuals whose
successful appearance makes them fear that some big
event will reveal them to be the very opposite. They are
afraid of being discovered as inadequate and lacking. The
label given to this fear is known as "The Imposter Phenomenon,"[3] a term coined from research among high
achievers, especially in our generation. It speaks of the
self-doubt that dogs the steps even of those like Grant,
who for all appearances should be free of such insecuri-
ties.

Grant's life is a good example of the kind of stress and

constant demand that many of us carry—stress that takes
its toll beneath well-fashioned appearances. Grant has a
clinic to supervise, professional groups to attend, a wife
and four children, and significant church involvement as
well. His wife tells him that he's pushing too hard. He
doesn't know how to relax. "I need some time to process
all that is happening around me," he says, "to sort
through my own affairs. But I rarely find such time, unless you count midnight till two a.m." Yet only those
closest to him would ever guess how stretched he feels.
He has years of professional bedside manner to disguise
his own uneasiness.

In her book *Passages*, Gail Sheehy explains why midlife is often marked by an inner restlessness and uncertainty.[4] Part of the reason we look more together than we
feel is that the middle years of life require us to do so
much personal reevaluation. It is the time of reassess-
ment. Have we done yet what we hoped to do? What
exactly were our original hopes and dreams, and how
does our life stack up against those measurements?

Sheehy quotes famous people from other eras to re-
mind us how universal this kind of interior struggle is.
There is Eleanor Roosevelt, who on her thirty-fifth birthday, complained that she never felt less confident in her
life. The philosopher Dante wrote that "in the middle of
his journey he came to a dark wood where the straight
way was lost."

Every generation has to deal with dashed dreams and
the confusion that often marks the process of growing
older. But for those of us born after World War II, in an
era of such inflated hopes, the task is even harder. Because our expectations were so high to begin with, we
have had much farther to fall. The letdown of facing life
as it is, instead of how you hoped it would be, is even
greater.

In my twenties I felt pretty near invincible, a kind of
religious 'I-am-woman-hear-me-roar.' The usual initia-

tory rites of adulthood had been easy enough to attain. I finished school, got married, put my husband through seminary while I taught, and, near the end of the school year, rushed to the hospital to deliver our first child. Hard work and determination could take you almost anywhere I thought.

Not until I was somewhere in my thirties did I recognize, in a personal sense, that I was struggling with inner feelings and doubts that did not always match the confident image I projected.

My wide-eyed enthusiasm, my own set of great expectations, began to disintegrate in the cold astringent of real life. The ministry for which my husband and I had seemingly spent years in preparation carried as many headaches and disappointments as joys. Our children were getting older and it was daily more evident that neither would grow up to be president. I began to see the frailty and humanness in some of my spiritual heroes, Christians I had looked up to in the past. The goals I had worked so hard to achieve only left me with more to reach for. I felt let down, as though the old sense of wonder and anticipation had completely evaporated from my life. I wanted to say, "You mean, this is the way life turns out? *This* is it? What have I missed? Surely there's more!" That was some of what was happening beneath the calm surface of my life. I appeared far more together than I felt on the inside.

ALONE IN A CROWD

Another characteristic of the postwar generation, as we find ourselves older and somewhat wiser, is that we are intensely aware of our longing for relationship; for a sense of connection with God, with other people, even with ourselves. Perhaps one explanation is that having been herded together from our youth the need and desire for strong relationships has been built in to us.

Whatever the reason, we have not achieved much of that desired goal. We are strangely lonely people. Like the song says in the sitcom, *Cheers,* it would be nice to go some place where everybody knows your name—if we could just find out where that is. Here especially, in this relational arena, reality has fallen far short of our expectations.

Jack Skeen, a Baltimore psychologist whose practice is innundated with individuals between twenty-five and forty-five, explains: "Almost to a person, there is a loneliness in this age group, a hungering to be understood. In spite of their accomplishments and their past relationships, they have rarely found anyone who understands that loneliness or acknowledges the part of them that's unique and personal. I think that in many ways they are a very powerless generation, easily swayed by advertising, yet because of their numbers, often overlooked as individuals."

The longing for intimacy can be the hidden motivation for much of what we have accomplished. Our culture seems to hold out the implicit promise that if you apply yourself—if you overcome this obstacle or that—the carrot at the end of the stick is shaped in the form of a person. If you chew Wrigley's gum you will double your pleasure and double your fun, and double your chances to meet an attractive woman. The goal behind the goal is a lasting, intimate relationship, a personal sense of *family.*

Yet therein is the rub. You can win the Nobel Prize and celebrate that fact essentially alone. There is little direct connection between accomplishment and relationship. "Many in this age group have indeed applied themselves," Skeen says, "only to realize through depression or marital problems or unrelenting singleness that all their hard work hasn't fulfilled the aching, lonely void of unmet relational needs. They long for someone to care about them as a person—to matter just for who they are."

"I haven't really had close friends since I was in high school," confides one editor in her early forties. "It's not that I wouldn't love to have some now, but I don't know who it's safe to talk to at work. You never know how people will read you or what they might repeat."

Another computer whiz who is also a single father says, "Sometimes I feel like I live in a state of emotional vertigo. Most of the time I'm just spinning around in circles, carrying out a list of tasks, connected to no one, really."

There is a kind of emotional, relational shriveling that takes place when our lives move so fast, and the stress is so heavy and thick that we cannot forge the friendships and connections we need. Many of us are long on associations and short on relationships. One pastor admits, "When the Million Dollar Roundtable of young business executives asked me to speak, I was amazed at the topic they requested. Friendships. These people can *do* all sorts of things but they don't know how to build lasting friendships."

An Episcopal priest agrees: "Most people in this generation live in their own isolated boxes in the suburbs, a thousand miles away from family, in communities in which they feel no roots. They are plagued by loneliness, yet driven by demanding jobs and competing family needs. Underneath all that activity is a deep longing for connection with God that seems real and intimate."

A person can be lonely inside the closest of relationships, but those who experience the demand and isolation of single parenting feel it quite acutely. By the turn of the century, more than half of our generation will have experienced divorce at least once, many more than once. Two-thirds of the children we gave birth to in the '80s will spend some time with a single parent.[5] The toll of single parenting—of singleness in general—brings its own sort of relational vacuum.

Susan's story is a classic case in point. When she was thinking of marrying Jim, that relationship symbolized certainty to her. She met him in college, in the context of a campus ministry and she hoped, as we all do, to gain a soul-mate, a friend, as well as a husband. She had never really known a woman who was a single mother raising children.

They hadn't been married very long, though, before real problems started to surface. "Within the first two years," Susan says, "I realized that Jim was battling a lot of old ghosts in his personal life. His relationship with his dad was a continual source of pressure for him. His compulsion to prove himself made him a driven man." It was like there were hidden reefs that blocked any real hope of being close.

Soon after they were married, Jim was elected president of his seminary class. He also became the youngest elder in their church. In many ways, Jim was simply too talented for his own good. No one realized that the image he put forth was incongruent with the man inside, or that his lifelong inability to gain his father's affirmation was an inner sore that still festered.

Jim's ministry continued to flourish, his outward performance serving to deflect attention from his inner needs. He confided in his pastor that he was struggling with an attraction to pornography, but his pastor didn't take him seriously. The church was growing so rapidly that Jim and Susan just got lost in the crowd.

Eventually, Jim decided to drop out of seminary and go back into the business world. But Susan suspected that his decision had not been as simple as it looked. Jim began to travel more and more in his job. Susan wondered if something was wrong, and when he began staying out half the night, becoming as emotionally distant as he was physically absent, she really started to worry.

The advice she received from other Christians was confusing, though. The implication was that if Susan could just be a better, sexier, more encouraging wife, her husband would return to his normal self. The only trouble was, hers didn't.

When Jim left—or more accurately, when Susan finally insisted that Jim get help and Jim left—more than a marriage and family was shattered. It would take a number of years to rebuild Susan's ability to trust people, to trust her own judgment, and to learn what it meant to trust God.

For more than ten years, Susan has been raising her two girls alone. "I've gotten over the tendency to be apologetic when I say I'm divorced," she says. "I am divorced and that's the reality of it all. And part of that reality is a kind of loneliness that creeps in—in little ways and big ways—in the way I sense my girls need a father. There is no one to share the load of responsibility for parenting two children, no one who can pick up for me when I get tired. Between my job and my children's activities there is little time left to pursue the kind of friendships that would provide more of the support I need at this point in my life. Loneliness is a persistent struggle for me—one that I live with in a daily way."

So with the challenges of singleness, of lives that move too fast, of relationships that produce acquaintances when we long for friendships, there are many in our generation who are painfully aware of feeling alone—even in a crowd.

DOWN THE UP ESCALATOR

Another way in which our lives are different than we expected is economically. The good times of the '50s and '60s became, for many, the tight times of the '70s and '80s. "I feel that there's a life I was raised to have," one man said, "and financially, I just haven't been able to make that happen." The subtitle of Christopher Lasch's 1979 best-seller *The Culture of Narcissism* reads: "American Life in an Age of *Diminishing Expectations*" (emphasis mine).

We have moved from the implicit promise of upward mobility to the stark possibility of going down the up escalator. The image of the Yuppie in a business suit sprinting up the courthouse steps, briefcase in hand, is largely a creation of the media. While his numbers will increase slightly in the '90s, there are many more of us who barely pay our bills. The majority of us will earn less, in real income, at every age than did the generation which preceded us. For those of us known as "younger boomers" (ages twenty-five to thirty-four), economic realities have been particularly harsh. Their house payments can be twice the size of the older group, their discretionary funds considerably less, and many of the best jobs gone before they got on the scene.

The guarantees in the system, real or implied, are no longer there. Instead, the cracks are widening and no amount of electric coffee grinders or compact disc players can prevent our falling through. Most of us have mortgages to pay and too much bought on plastic. In a few short years, the hot career field of today may be overcrowded and obsolete. In fact, most people in this age group will shift into new careers, not once or twice, but more than three times over a lifetime.

No matter how hard we try, most of us have not been able to recreate the safe, tidy lives that we remember our parents having. Though we are the largest group of college-educated Americans ever, that statistic may have served only to line the entrance lobby with far too many applicants for the job we wanted.

It seemed so easy—too easy, maybe—for our parents' generation, as though they collectively possessed the Midas Touch. In the 25 years that followed World War II, our parents saw their real purchasing power double, a phenomenon not seen before or since. I remember one likeable man in my hometown, the local football coach, who made a smooth transition from football into selling millions of dollars of life insurance to returning WWII veterans. Another, a local banker, built a modest apartment building on low interest rates. When he retired, he sold those twelve units for more than he made in a lifetime at his regular profession. You have to work very hard to recount stories like that in our generation.

Ted, the same guy who recruited half his fraternity to hear a Christian speaker in college, was not prepared for the uphill struggle he encountered in the floral business. Friends had always told him that he had a natural gift for making money. By the age of twenty-five, when most guys can barely think beyond the upcoming weekend, Ted was busy buying small houses during the real estate boom of the '70s.

Hard work had never been a stranger to him. Though he could have rested in his parent's affluence, he was the son who found his own job in a paint store at fourteen. He had grown up expecting to work hard, and he had grown up expecting that hard work to pay off well.

The fact that Ted had become a Christian in college only deepened his desire to go into business. He used to daydream about how he wanted to be part of a whole collection of businessmen committed to incarnating their witness in what was often a competitive, compromising environment.

The floral business was a natural match for Ted's abilities. He started out packing boxes with flowers at the largest wholesale florist in Chicago; within a few years he managed an entire division. Like a walking inventory sheet, he had a rare ability to store mammoth amounts of numbers in his head. Yet he was a real salesman as well, as comfortable with people as he was with invoices.

Ted sailed through his first year of owning his own business. Inside, he couldn't help congratulating himself just a little. He felt like he was on the verge of laying hold of a long-awaited dream.

Then, in what seemed like only the time it takes to feel the wind shift, everything changed. A cloud of unemployment and business slowdown began to envelop what had previously been a prosperous region. Suddenly consumers thought they could do without flowers. The floral shops who were Ted's clients began placing smaller and smaller orders.

"When I first went to the bank to see about a loan for this business," Ted says, "there was another man waiting as well, and he had been in business for two years. Right away he started telling me about employees who wanted to sue him, about his problems with computers and the IRS and tax people and lawyers, about his struggles with cash flow, collections, and sleep. I thought to myself, 'Boy, I can't relate to this at all.' "

Ted looks back on that conversation now as having been somewhat prophetic, as he soon discovered what it was like to have everything he touched turn to ashes— not gold. He is only one of many whose career and financial goals have been downsized by a shrinking economy and abrupt reversals of fortune; whose secret fear is that they may go down what was supposed to be an up escalator.

GAINING PERSPECTIVE

"You've come a long way, baby," sang the Virginia Slims commercials. Indeed, we have. Within a little more than two decades we have seen many of our great expectations and big dreams evaporate before our eyes. We have both inherited and created a world much more complex and uncertain than we expected. As columnist P. J. O'Rourke wrote, " 'We are the world,' we shouted just a couple of years ago. And just a couple of years ago we were. How did we wind up so old? So fat? So confused? So broke?"[6]

Twenty-five years ago, those of us in "Sunday school," had dreams that were linked—in a veiled way—to our understanding of God and what it meant to follow him. We were introduced to an all-powerful God; not some nebulous entity devoid of definition, but a God who had invaded history in the person of Jesus Christ, a God who could be known. The times in which we were living and the way we heard the message meant that, in many cases, we only believed all the more deeply that our goals and dreams would be reached. The fact that our lives were linked to the God of the universe was like wind beneath our feet allowing us to soar in life where others stalled. We would leap where others only stumbled along. "God loved us and had a wonderful plan for our lives," and our belief in him seemed to put us in a special category of immunity and protection. In our youthful minds, there was no understanding of or preparation for hardships that refused to go away and pain that required time to heal. As a result, our disappointments have often been experienced even more deeply than those of our unbelieving brothers and sisters.

Like Susan and Ted and me—even Grant in less obvious ways—divorce and business failures, insecurity and dissatisfaction were not part of our mental concept of the abundant life in Christ. Consequently, we have found the task of sorting out old dreams and coming to terms with life, as we near and pass the age of "frantic forty," to be a much greater challenge than we would have thought.

That sorting-out process, so common to anyone between the ages of thirty-five and forty-five, requires that we look back into our past as well as forward into our future. It is similar to what it feels like to come to the crest of a hill and look in both directions while standing still at the top. For those of us whose dreams were even loosely attached to our faith, the need to look backward is even more imperative.

Indeed, where we are now as individuals—and in a larger sense, as a generation—is rooted in where we have been. Our childhoods and the era known as the '60s played a huge role in establishing the foundation from which we experienced the disappointments that have come since. There, amidst hula hoops and super-heroes, we birthed our great expectations.

CHAPTER 4

The Children of Promise

Tracing the Birth of Those Great Expectations

We consciously think of ourselves as different from those people who came before.

Walt Harrison, 41

———————————◆———————————

On a cloudless afternoon two summers ago, I boarded a plane bound for Minneapolis. In no time the plane climbed to its proper cruising altitude and I sat back in my seat and relaxed. It was a perfect day for flying.

By the time our plane neared Minneapolis I was lost in conversation with a nine-year-old Malaysian boy, fluent in English, who told me everything I had ever wanted to know about his country—and then some. I failed to notice just how long we had been circling the airport, or the strained silence of the passengers. Just as I started to feel vaguely nauseous—you can only go around in circles so long—we began our descent.

The plane touched ground, and curiously enough, spontaneous applause rippled through the passengers. What a warm, responsive group, I thought. Little white trucks with strobe red lights lined the runway beside our plane. How remarkable. This conscientious airport had fire drills even on Sundays.

Not until I got to baggage claim and chanced to overhear another passenger say he was just glad to be alive did I start to suspect anything. I ventured a naive question: "Pardon me, but I was on that plane. Was there something wrong?"

He peered at me over his beard like I had been locked

in the restroom with my headphones on. "Lady," he said, in carefully measured words. "Lady, didn't you hear that pilot? The plane's wheels wouldn't come down for a full half hour. We almost landed in that field out there." I gathered my bags—a little sheepishly, I admit—and headed down the concourse, thankful that I *hadn't* heard what the pilot said. In the back of my mind, echoes from the past, voices of the little rascals in my original neighborhood, reminded me that I was something of a space cadet after all.

I am still amazed that I could have spent the last hour of that trip so thoroughly unaware of the predicament I was in. Surely there had been enough airplane disasters to make one wary. Yet somehow my unbridled optimism remained intact. I successfully overlooked even the most obvious warning signs because I had never expected to encounter anything but an uneventful ride, a smooth sail to where I wanted to go.

In the past few years, as I've observed the disillusionment many of us face in midlife, the analogy of that plane ride often comes to mind. When we started out, the prospects for the future were sunny, hopeful, reassuring. We were flying the friendly skies of Eisenhower or Kennedy's America. Wars and recessions were part of the past; few prophets foresaw a shrinking economy or the pressures that would fall on families of the '90s. There seemed to be little reason to warn of potential disaster.

Every group of 20 year olds has stars in their eyes, big dreams, and great hopes for the future. But for our generation, the good times of the '50s and '60s made for an even greater sense of expectation, an illusion of guarantees. This was the buildup that led to such a letdown and to frustration that simmers just beneath the surface.

We have encountered far more turbulence than we planned for on this trip: dissolving marriages, double-digit inflation, job scarcity, internal stress, and persistent loneliness that our parents' generation would have hardly imagined. It's shaky out there—and sometimes it's a bit shaky "in here" too.

CHILDHOOD COCOONS

When you set out to discover where and how you first formed notions about what you could expect on this flight through life, you inevitably find yourself sorting through the relics of your childhood. There, surrounded by Mickey Mouse hats and Beatles records, we formed many of our impressions about what we could expect out of life.

Social researchers point out that somewhere around your tenth year, your values and outlook, your expectations, are forged into definable shape. Between the ages of ten and twenty you just test and confirm your original values. After that, it will require considerable pain or payoff to move those values out of their locked-in places.

Young eyes and minds absorb far more than they appear to. It's as though you take a hard look at what's happening around you, digest the messages coming from TV, your parents, the kid next door, and you say, "This is the way life *is*. This is the way life will be."

Do you remember where you were and what you were doing at the tender age of ten? Can you focus in on that slice of your life and interpret what you surmised about the world from those relationships and circumstances?

When I play back the tape of memories in my mind, I stop on a warm spot around my tenth year and find myself sitting beside the red clay bank that surrounded our home, a gallon pickle jar of water beside me. There on the side of the mountain, I would sit for hours, with the sun warming my back as I molded pots out of the Indian dirt. I loved the squishy, malleable quality of the clay, the way it took shape beneath the pressure of my fingers. I think that image accurately summarizes my childhood assumptions about life itself. I believed that with enough skill and effort on my part, the forces and events of my life could be shaped as readily as that red clay.

But I wasn't alone on this hill. About ten of us ran together as a herd all over the side of that mountain, making hideouts deep in the woods, oblivious to the thought of danger. "Crime" was limited, in our minds, to the streets of Harlem, a mythical evil necessary to thicken the plot of Dragnet.

Occasionally, we checked in with our mothers, none of whom were June Cleavers, but they were there, present, maybe even too involved in their children's lives. And divorce? There were no children from single parent homes on our hill. Parents might have argued a bit, in those days, but divorce—that word wasn't common to our relational vocabularies until much later. Whatever might have actually been missing from our family relationships (and judging from the current number of ACoA and sexual abuse support groups, it was quite a lot), on the surface at least, the image of togetherness held intact.

Susan looks back on her childhood as a period of life that was almost too good to be true. Her Dad made a comfortable living managing a local chain of bookstores in a community where family roots were measured not in years but in generations, where no one locked their doors unless they left for a two-week vacation. She admits her family relationships were shallow, but most difficulties were hidden beneath a pleasant, effective veneer that served to protect her from the messier, more painful side of life.

She is grateful for the good times of her childhood. But she is quick to add that her sheltered background only made the hard knocks of divorce doubly difficult to take. "I realize now how unprepared I was for life," Susan says. "My marriage falling apart was the first major incidence in my life of realizing that not everyone you trust deserves such trust. After Jim left, I felt like I'd been catapulted out of a cocoon.''

So while our bright childhoods were probably more image than substance, that aura of security and privilege shaped our expectations for the future. Even now, when we flip the radio dial to the nostalgia music of that era, it's the magic, as much as the music, that draws us.

DIFFERENT CHILDHOODS, DIFFERENT VALUES

We need only compare our parents' orientation (The War Generation) with our own (The Boom Generation) to realize that a person's early perceptions of life filter his whole outlook. Never has so much diversity existed simultaneously in the same century, affording us, as a result, the chance to observe how important those early experiences really are.[1]

The fine irony is that our parents' experience has been practically the reverse of our own. The hardest years of their lives were, for the most part, the first years of their lives—the proving ground from which they moved on to better things. They may have grown up in the Great Depression and fought in World War II, but when they returned they were able to build lives that, for many, were beyond their wildest hopes.

Yet we have to ask, Didn't our parents encounter disappointments, too, as they moved from adolescence to adulthood? Didn't they have dreams and illusions they were forced to let go of? Undoubtedly, they did. Every generation has its pipe dreams. Youthful idealism, it's called. But in their case, the two major events of their childhood and adolescence came to their aid. The Depression and World War II taught them that hardship and sacrifice were just a few of many unpleasant possibilities that might come a person's way. Life was not easy.

Because of their earlier experiences, they were more informed of reality. The Great Depression was more than a story handed down from the generation before—they lived through it. They watched or were among the able-bodied young men leaving for the shores of the Pacific or the battlefields of Europe, many of whom would never return.

So while the War Generation, as every generation before, left adolescence harboring its own set of dreams, those dreams were tempered by previous experience, and as a result, they were better able to deal with life as it came to them. Whatever let-down they experienced was less pronounced. For one thing, many of their dreams materialized, and even when some didn't, the discrepancy between their dreams and reality was not as great as ours.

Our Parents' Values

Our parents' early memories are filled with the haggard faces of men in search of work. They lived with scarcity and need and the insecurity of not knowing whether the family would have to "sell the farm" or move to a whole new community to find work. As the result of the hard times they grew up in, where a person could hardly plan for the future because the present was so tenuous, the War Generation has always placed a high premium on *stability.* They are more cautious and conservative, unwilling to count any chickens before they hatch. There is a right way to worship and raise children. Everything has a place and needs to be there. Predictability and security are paramount.

Where our generation has accentuated the distinctiveness of the individual, our parents have placed a higher value on *the power of the group.* It took a team effort to pull out of the Depression and to win a war. Such mammoth tasks were only accomplished by everyone pulling together. The individual sublimated his own desires in favor of a larger need; he put his shoulder to the wheel now and asked questions later. And any good team has a strong leader as implicitly trustworthy as Dwight Eisenhower or Douglas MacArthur. For our parents, commitment to authority and institutions have been givens since their childhoods.

They have been criticized for not taking the time to smell the roses, but nothing in their formative years allowed for such leisure. *Hard work* has prevailed as the queen of virtues for their age group and it's no wonder, since it was work, work, and more work that got them out of two tight jams and eventually ushered in an era of unprecedented prosperity.

GREAT BEGINNINGS

Unfortunately, we would have to take our parents' childhoods and life experiences and turn them upside down if we wanted to match our own. The best years of our lives have been, for the most part, the first years of our lives. [2] There was little reason at that point to think that the future held anything except more and better of the same. It is for good reason that the Hebrew wisdom of the Old Testament states that "it is good for a man to bear the yoke while he is young." [3] We are better off if life goes from worse to better, rather than from better to worse.

When Ted speaks of his own background he explains how he grew up hearing his parents' stories about how hard life was in the Depression and how hard they worked all their lives. "That's exactly where I got my impression that all my hard work would pay off as handsomely for me as theirs did for them," he says. Ted was raised in a Dutch family in New England where for generations father had passed onto son the virtues of thrift and labor.

Just as surely as the cart always follows the horse, each generation of the family has grown a bit more prosperous for the effort. Except for Ted. He had no reference point to prepare him for hard work where the payoff was simply keeping himself just inches in front of his creditors.

When we think of the factors in our childhoods that fueled our great expectations, one holds particular influence: our numbers. There were just so very many of us. We had new elementary schools, new textbooks, new station wagons, all bought or built to accommodate record numbers of children produced in the wake of America's victory euphoria.

Our size made us an irresistibly large market, tracked by invisible little guys with clipboards (market researchers they were called), who followed us around, noting our preferences. On their advice, the forests were denuded in search of raccoon tails for Davy Crockett hats. Their commercial savvy gave us little plastic rings called "hula hoops," producing as many as twenty million a day until one month in 1959, the market turned and you couldn't give a hula hoop away. Seventy-six million babies, toddlers, school children and teenagers—a huge spotlight was focused on this bulging herd of humanity.

So, imperceptibly, the preferences of our generation began to dominate. Instead of adopting our parents' choices and opinions, we established our own. Mass-produced hamburgers, Weejuns, and miniskirts were tailored to our tastes. We made rock music everyone's music. We danced to it, got married to it, and from all accounts, those of us who can afford to will sit retired on Florida beaches and tap our arthritic toes to it. Whatever the item, if we liked it, someone got rich—when we cast it aside, someone went broke.

That is a lot of power to rest in the hands of one group of people. When McDonald's told us that we needed a break today and Burger King said we could have it our way, we knew they were singing our song. We ate instant oatmeal and watched Polaroid pictures develop before our eyes. Television, that ubiquitous metal and glass box in the corner of the living room, deceptively portrayed a lifestyle that was, in fact, three times the average American income. In sixty minutes any personal or global problem could be solved, and if you were bored, you simply changed the channel. We were children with endless options and our choices came in 31 flavors.

One stray piece of generational trivia among many helps explain why we grew up expecting life to go better than it has. An unusual proportion of us were firstborns, eldest children who are able for a brief sparkling moment to claim the center of their parent's attention. But as one commentator notes, the prevailing emphasis on children made a whole generation "eldest children," growing up with the idea that the "world is organized just for them."[4] We felt *entitled* to the good life. What other generations had thought of as privileges—sending your children to college, a secure retirement, for instance—appeared to us to be rights.

In addition to a sense of entitlement, research on birth order suggests that the first-born is also likely to trust authority more deeply, to believe that life is very orderly and the world is just. Firstborns are usually quite conscientious and instinctively expect to be rewarded for their efforts.

"I felt that I was entitled to a whole lot in life," says one midwestern mother of two. "I was the only girl amidst three brothers and I felt very special. We lived in a nice parsonage; my family was center-stage at church.

"I remember reading in *Weekly Readers* about how we would all have helicopters. And because somebody had just invented space food, we wouldn't even have to eat. If we wanted to be President of the United States, then we could. When I was in high school, I didn't pay any attention to cheerleading and home ec—I took drafting and electronics. There was never any doubt in my mind that I could do anything I wanted to. All doors were open to me."

Gone were the days when children existed to contribute to the family struggle for survival. Unlike our parents, who were thankful to get oranges and apples in their Christmas stockings, Santa Claus could bring us most anything in the Sears and Roebuck Catalog. Most parents strove to spare their children the austerity of their own childhoods—though not without a little instructive recall, now and then.

I remember how my mother used to describe the four miles she walked to school through the treacherous Virginia mountains. That long-ago-and-far-away glaze would cover her eyes and you knew what was coming.

"Don't you realize," she would say, forgetting how well I realized, "that I used to walk four miles one way every day, in cold, wind, snow, sleet, and hail to get to school?"

My brother and I she drove.

The Values of the Postwar Generation

Growing up in such a different era caused our values and outlook to differ greatly from our parents. Because of our size and numbers, following our *own* dream has long been crucial for us. The question constantly in the back of our minds is, "What kind of individual contribution can I make?" Visibility, recognition, impact, and accomplishment are the things we value.

Grant, the psychiatrist, knows what that drive to stand out in a crowd is like. "On the one hand," he says, "I watched the example of my father and took note. He held a steady government job all his life, one where the promotions and raises followed like clock work. Part of me just thought I'd grow up and take my place on the dog sled—no meteoric, rising star. Yet I have to admit that underneath those lame ambitions, there is the churning to do something remarkable. I'd like to cut a path that has been overlooked. I want to leave my own mark."

Grant claims that the longing to soar rather than just coast along is part of what propelled him into medical school and made him one of the youngest psychiatrists in his class to establish his own clinic. Yet he finds that for each goal he reaches, a new one crops up in front of him. On the other hand, the older he gets the more he sees the need to slow down, enjoy where he is, and declare enough is enough.

As individuals, we also tend to feel less compelled to melt into the standard conventions prescribed by a larger group. More often we follow an internal drummer, in tune with our own instincts. The question, *Why?* is second nature. Our parents rose to the occasion when a patriotic man with a pointed finger said, "Uncle Sam wants you!" Our generation replied, "Heck, no, I won't go."

We also seem to have been on a long and roundabout search to *find meaning in life.* Beneath all the drivenness to accumulate more and bigger, we still long to grab hold of what matters—what really matters. The search for fulfillment continues and the options multiply.

Because of that searching nature, we welcome change and variation, not as something to be feared, but to be taken advantage of. We have a low threshold for boredom. Whether it's a winter ski vacation or serving lunch in a downtown soup kitchen, we are prone to collect experiences like our parents collected coins. We embrace the new and different, always on the look-out for what adds meaning and purpose to life.

THE IMPACT OF THE SIXTIES

Most commentators feel our childhoods were special, and that those childhoods left us with the *feeling* of being special as well. You may remember the moment in *The Big Chill* when actor William Hurt, the resident philosopher, turns to his middle-aged friends and says, "Wise up, guys, no one ever had a cushier birth."

It is just this "cushy birth," with its inherent sense of privilege, that fueled much of the idealism of The Sixties.

From the charmed childhoods most of us had, we moved right on into a decade as schizophrenic as any this century has known. Differing stories were simultaneously played out before our eyes, like two competing television screens. One picture showed millions of us packing our bags for college, feeding off America's affluence and world position.

But the other screen was red and bleeding like an open wound, throbbing with the pain of Vietnam, of civil rights demonstrations, and the deaths of heroes. The scenes that invaded our sanitized living rooms—angry protesters and naked Vietnamese children—challenged the surface tranquility of our lives. We were caught between the sense of standing on the threshold of fulfilling big dreams and the nagging awareness that some sinister force was astir.

Because a person's perspective on that era varies with the picture they were most tuned into, there will always be room for differing opinions. In fact, when *Newsweek* correspondent Tom Matthews prophesies the future, he half-humorously envisions that fifty years from now, when there are only a couple dozen centenarians left, "the last liberal and the last conservative, the last lieutenant and the last draft-card burner, the last head and the last narc will undoubtedly be out on the porch at the Home trying to gum each other to death over the Last Principle."[5] There will still be memories and viewpoints to discuss.

There is a lot that could be said about the Sixties, yet one theme remains constant. Beneath the clamor and the dissonance, a note of idealism holds steady. In spite of Vietnam and the assassinations of three national figures, our belief that we could win the day stayed intact. Not until the exposure of Watergate in 1972 did we start to settle back in our armchairs with a sigh of apathy, eventually fading into disillusionment.

Until then, it seemed that we could get around gravity —if we were clever enough. Listen to *Time* magazine's 1967 assessment of our potential: "In its lifetime, this promising generation could land on the moon, cure cancer and the common cold, lay out blight-proof, smog-free cities, help end racial prejudice, enrich the underdeveloped world and, no doubt, write an end to poverty and war."[6] About the only thing left out of that list is the ability to walk on water.

To live through this era was to absorb, as if by osmosis, an optimism that fed our already over-sized hopes and expectations for what life could deliver. With enough protest, or by sheer force of will, age-old social ills could be remedied. The problems that other generations had tried to chip away piece by piece, we clamored to undo overnight. This was the Age of Aquarius—the dawning of a new day.

That idealism was also easy to transport. We carried it into our understanding of Christianity with some wonderful, and some not so wonderful, results. In some ways, that heady sense of being on the front end of a tidal wave aided the Christian cause. It served to emphasize the radical nature of the gospel. *Now* was the time to make a decision for Christ, and that decision was life-changing. A person's commitment mattered; his life could make a difference in a world that needed that difference.

The intensity with which those ideas were embraced left little doubt as to the crucial importance of the claims of Christ. "When I told my parents I had become a Christian," one pastor recalls, "they said that they had just lost a son. And that hurt. But it also made me dig for answers. I realized that if the gospel was true then it affected every area of my life—my school work, my ambitions for the future, my relationship with my parents. I saw that I was staring in the face of the most significant life questions a person has to deal with."

Likewise, the great hopes we held in common produced a bonding, a web of relationships not easily equaled or surpassed. Many of us still count our friendships from that era among the closest we've ever experienced.

INFLATED DREAMS

But there was a dark side to that idealism as well. It also carried in its wake a number of false hopes and pipe dreams. Inevitably, the big build-up had its own kind of letdown. The most obvious of these took place en masse. We didn't change the world—all that much. Our global dreams were forced to shrink.

A half million people gathered in a farmer's field in Woodstock, their lighted candles swaying in the dark as they tried to hurry along this new era with all the emotional fervor of a religious revival. But the new day that dawned was pretty much the same as those that went before. Folk singer Arlo Guthrie prophesied that all political systems were on the way out, that we were finally going to get to the point where there would be no more bigotry or war. But racism and enmity proved as hard to stamp out as brush fires in a dry forest.

Not long after Woodstock, 100,000 Christians gathered in the Cotton Bowl in Dallas, Texas for a week called Explo '72, an event heralded as the most significant Christian happening since Pentecost. By day they sat under the broiling Texas sun, and at night they sang along with the best Christian music groups and listened to spirited messages. Afterwards they stuck to the seats of crowded buses that carried them to remote suburbs to sleep on air mattresses in empty apartments—and they thought little of it.

They were part of a "conspiracy" to change the world,

an army of Christians who could, by 1980, fulfill Christ's Great Commission to take the gospel to every single person. We were going to change the world in our generation. *In our generation.* Remember?

A noble task in a needy world—that's the stuff dreams are made of. "When I look back on that era as a Christian," one educator says, "I realize what a simplistic view of the spheres of power we had. We thought we could make whatever changes needed to be made. There were no real problems that wouldn't go away." If we were clever enough, we could subdue gravity.

For many of us, the idealism that had been focused on global change also spilled over into our personal lives, as in Susan's case. Her hopes took the shape of a relationship—a stable, intimate marriage. That was the desire of her heart and one that seemed in alignment with what God would want as well. "Part of the protective bubble I lived in then," she says, "was the idea that if my dreams were good, real pain and heartache wouldn't touch me. Not deeply, anyway. The emphasis was on trusting God to work everything out, so I didn't ask too many questions beyond that. Every circumstance in my life just seemed to point to marrying Jim."

That same idealism caused us to skip lightly over the harder words of Scripture that spoke of surrender and adversity, of failure and weakness. Our backgrounds left us unprepared for some of the irreversible losses, the painful letting go that comes with growing up and growing older in a fallen world.

Our communal dreams were accompanied by personal assumptions, our youthful illusions smuggled in until the gospel became, in part, a golden thread that would help tie up the loose ends of our lives in a neat package. We connected our personal dreams and our mental images of the good life with mustard-seed faith in a God who could move mountains. Many of our high hopes were overlaid with Bible promises, and therein lies a double sting. The Apostle Paul said that God was able to do exceedingly abundantly beyond all we could ask or think. What such mammoth assurances meant to a generation of Christians with oversized aspirations, only God knows.

If he was going to do exceedingly abundantly for us, then he was in for a challenge.

Part II

Letting Go of Old Dreams

CHAPTER 5

Broken Rainbows

Acknowledging the Promises God Never Made

The idea I absorbed was that if you did what God said, everything would come out all right in the end. What I found, though, is that the end may be a lot further down the road than you think.

Paul Borthwick, 37

━━━━━━━━━━━━ ◆ ━━━━━━━━━━━━

For the first few years after I turned 30 I was aware of a vague feeling of disappointment—a kind of general malaise, with few observable symptoms and no name. It just turned up unpredictably, here and there, like recurrent mono. Or to change the metaphor, it simmered on the back burner in my mind, and as long as I kept the heat turned down, I was O.K.

It was not as though something catastrophic had taken place. At the time, my husband and I were leading a collegiate ministry at a university in Oklahoma. We were hoping to see some of those students gain a heart for ministering overseas, but realizing slowly that, if you're a kid who has grown up in Oklahoma, Little Rock is a foreign country.

But there was plenty to keep a person encouraged, and for the most part, I was too busy chasing toddlers and squirreling away a few hours behind a typewriter to devote much energy to introspection. I only knew, deep down, that there was a widening gap between what I had hoped for and what was actually happening in my life, and that the disillusionment had something to do with God.

That part I hated to admit. It took me a long time to see that my disappointment was tangled up with my ideas about the Christian life. Besides, the fact that I was married to a man in the ministry was a complicating factor. In that role I often felt cast as a kind of spiritual presswoman doing public relations work for God. And that is one odd spot to be in when you are having second thoughts yourself. I couldn't understand why the "abundant life" that seemed to promise so much more—more intimacy, more impact, more satisfaction—had, in many instances, mysteriously turned out to be less.

I decided to treat my life like a video and play a few scenes backward, until I could find those private places where I had first formed mental images of how I had expected things to turn out. Only then did I discover how much my faith had been influenced by my great expectations.

THE ABUNDANT LIFE?

There is one particularly creative episode of the award-winning show *thirtysomething* where every scene is followed by the scene that actually preceded it—a one hour drama played backwards. The analogy is intriguing.

The story begins in a hospital delivery room with Suzanne trying to give birth to a baby in no hurry to be born. Gary, the ungainfully-employed English professor, frets helplessly at her side. Women in transition are not pleasant company. He wipes the sweat from her face and tries to ignore her comment that she hates him for getting her pregnant in the first place. Yes, he will most certainly turn off Pachebel before she jumps right through the window. And the doctor sighs in exasperation. This patient stops pushing at the most crucial moments. It is not a pretty sight.

Amazingly, what follows is not two delighted parents gazing in wonder at the child of their love's creation.

Instead, the story moves backward. You see Gary and Suzanne with her swollen belly, back in their apartment gathering the essentials for the perfect birth. Slight contractions, mild and irregular, interrupt the process on occasion.

They arrive at the hospital with everything in hand—stereo, a book to read when bored, an old homey shirt to replace a sterile hospital gown, and a request for a room with a view. Suzanne props herself up in bed as though getting ready to order breakfast from room service, and in her tenderest of voices, dispenses Gary to make phone calls.

The real stuff comes later.

For any couple who has been through a childbirth experience together, the story on the screen is captivating. It's too funny, too true. As most couples know, it is one thing to anticipate the perfect childbirth and quite another to experience the real event.

The spiritual journey of our generation was similar, only we were rehearsing for the birth of our own lives as adults. We had our preconceived notions as well. In many cases, we prepared for events that took place much differently than we thought they would. For instance, when someone spoke of the abundant life to be found in Christ, what images formed in our minds? *In a large sense, those expectations revolved primarily around ideas of protection and guarantee.*

Somewhere in the idea of the "abundant life" in Jesus was a strong hint of a solution to most every problem, unhampered opportunities, untroubled relationships—a life that was largely wrinkle-free if only you found the right Bible study or appropriate spiritual principle. Missing were hard words like perseverance and loneliness and defeat. Christianity was seen not so much as a calling to a holy life as an invitation to a better one—an abundant life.

One woman reflects on the way she mixed her dreams

with notions about God this way: "I was so thoroughly schooled in the idea that God loved me and had a wonderful plan for my life that I was shocked, really shocked, when the first major unwonderful event took place." Another man adds, "I took a lot of false comfort in what I call the one-right-way illusion. If faced with a difficult decision, I had only to take my Bible and like a spiritual Thoreau, retire to Walden Pond. There I would lay out the options and God would show me the supremely right one, a sort of yellow brick road that, once followed, would guarantee me of never being wrong." Somehow, it seemed, if we just Christianized our ideals we could insure them.

Such ideas did not just materialize out of thin air. Way back in the fifties, Norman Vincent Peale contended in his best selling book *The Power of Positive Thinking* that the Bible contained "techniques" and "formulas" that formed an exact science on how to handle your problems. There were "ten simple, workable rules" for living and "magic words" that could overcome most anything.

By the time most of us reached our twenties, when we were trying to find our way through a new world of work and weddings and wet diapers, the pragmatic American mindset had thoroughly taken hold. Now there was a how-to seminar or Christian self-help book for nearly everything imaginable. If you wanted to follow a charted course of progress in Christian discipleship, there were workbooks that packaged those answers in "ten basic steps."[1] Did you need to know how to choose a mate or manage your finances or develop a biblical worldview? There was a method or program to help you. And if you followed the rules, you could count on success.

It's not as though there weren't plenty of biblical examples of men and women who never reached a pinnacle of success, whose lives mirrored perennial failure and hardship. We knew that Abraham had wandered around in tents all his life, and Stephen had been stoned to death. But I think many people heard stories like these the way I did. Somewhere in some tiny crevice of my mind, I explained those examples away. They belonged to another day—before the advent of American Express and lawyers with briefcases and power ties. Those models did not inform my great expectations because I had a filter in place.

Embarking on the Christian life, as it was oversold then and is still often presented, was something like looking through a travel brochure for a tropical island vacation. Each four-color page held a spread of inviting images: attractive accommodations, cheerful fellow-passengers, and charming sights, all reasonably priced.

The actual excursion, though, is markedly different than the brochure advertised. There are detours and setbacks; some much-anticipated events have been canceled altogether. And the price is greater than most of us imagined.[2]

Ted, for instance, never envisioned the humbling process of having to ask his creditors to accept a slower schedule of repayment. When he heard other businessmen discuss the financial climate of his city, somehow Ted expected that God would protect him from feeling the full effect of the economic downturn. He knew he had a lot to learn about the floral business, but hoped against hope that God would cover his tracks and make up for his lack of knowledge.

Grant spent his early years as a Christian focused on establishing all the right Christian habits. He regularly shared his faith with his unbelieving friends; rarely did he ever miss a day reading the Bible. All his life he had been the kind of person who did what he was supposed to do when he was supposed to do it. He thought that if he played by the rules, everyone else would as well. He was unprepared for employees who fudged on the amount of vacation days they had taken, or colleagues across town who made such bold efforts to build their practices at the expense of everyone else's.

The word "divorce" was not really in Susan's vocabulary until the prospect became imminent. Christians worked things out—they didn't divorce. Susan's image of herself was that of a supportive wife, a woman whose primary means of serving God was being a good wife and mother. She felt deeply defeated by divorce. Learning what it meant to honor God and to trust him in a role foreign to her thinking, that of a single parent, was a process she had never expected to encounter.

It is in our thirties that such idealism starts to break down. In a decade marked for many people by mini-losses and letting go—when your job or your marriage or your illusions of personal grandeur wear thin—the real begins to replace the caricature.[3] We begin to grapple with life as it really is and to understand—often only in retrospect—the illusions with which we began.

THE FALL OUT

For those whose great expectations of life went hand in hand with their great expectations of God, the fall-out has left its mark. The emotional residue alone has taken longer to shake off than some of the original false notions themselves.

False Guilt

One of the more common scars is false guilt—guilt when your life did not measure up, when after taking the tenth basic step to spiritual maturity you were still stumbling around. "I used to spend the best part of the weekend getting high on marijuana and cocaine until I became a Christian," says a budding college professor. "I think I tried Christianity something like I would have tried a new drug. My friends had said, 'Try Jesus. Jesus can take you higher than cocaine.' I did. They were wrong."

In short order, this man decided that whoever came up with that idea had never tried cocaine. He gave himself a year or so, waded his way into all the spiritual activities and programs his friends said would make his life better, and then quietly began to do a few drugs on the side.

He explains, "If that program I was following was supposed to alleviate any real struggles or problems I was experiencing, then I decided I must be doing the Christian life wrong. I felt like one big fake." Those little dots of peace and gentleness and joy that were supposed to line up around the edge of his circle if Jesus was on the throne were, instead, dancing in stubborn disarray.

He admits that the guilt of not having his life completely together would have driven him back to drugs had he not met a few people who were better models of authenticity. They weren't captive to the notion that their struggles would disappear if they mastered the right spiritual techniques. He discovered that Jesus could take him higher, but only if the definition of high didn't include feeling no pain.

"There must be something wrong with me." That is one of the easiest conclusions to draw when spirituality is cast in terms of the ability to transcend a difficulty, when there are "steps" and "secrets" to a higher plane. If there are eight steps to moral freedom, for instance, and at the end of the eighth you are still struggling with untamed lust, the guilt is enormous.

Where did we lose Martin Luther's description of the Christian life: not one of perpetual confidence, but rather the process of a recovering drunk who climbs on one side of the horse only to fall off the other side, get up and go at it again?

Larger-than-life expectations create their own kind of pressure. We cannot just be a person-in-process. We must be fixed. So relates a man who tried to get rid of colitis for five years: "For a large part of my twenties," he explains, "I had this embarrassing physical problem that everybody knew came from anxiety and stress. It was like wearing a badge of spiritual defeat for me. I read every book, attended every seminar I could find, but little changed. Honestly, the guilt of not being together was worse than the disease."

False Pretenses

When the Christian faith is oversold, those who know their lives are lacking retreat into hiding. Or at least they learn how to keep any of the messier parts well out of sight. It is amazing, ironic actually, that a religion built on truth could be so used to foster pretense.

"For a long time I used to tell people how the grace of God had kept me from being deeply affected by my father's abandonment and my stepfather's abuse," one woman in her early thirties says. "I learned pretty quick what was and was not permissible to share. People wanted to see me as a collected competent Christian and I let them. The only problem was that I stayed stuck emotionally and spiritually right where I was. It took me years to muster the personal courage to get honest about my past."

A pastor relates how he always likened his early Christian experience to that of Cinderella living in a palace.[4] Much of the emotional turmoil and depression that came from growing up in an alcoholic family had virtually evaporated. Later, things began to fray around the edges.

An unnerving level of personal defeat plagued him. Fears of dying and speaking in public (one as scary as the other) remained present tense in his life. How do you share with someone, if you're a pastor, that the thought of a pulpit is not too unlike a coffin, that death and preaching are synonymous and filled with fear? "The more I kept my struggles a secret," he admits now, "the more phobic I became. Yet I held back from honest sharing because I felt that if I were only more godly, I wouldn't have these struggles in the first place." It took him a long time to realize the recurring struggles that made his life more like a battleground than a palace were simply a legitimate part of the Christian life.

Only when we realize that heaven is the place reserved for perfection and final completeness can we live without false pretense here on earth.

A False Contract

Perhaps every generation, in its own way, faces the temptation to reduce a faith full of mystery and ambiguity and wonder to something a bit more manageable. It appears to be safer that way. As a result, we codify and concretize a God who insists on bursting our categories, who insists on surprising us.

The simplest way to box God in, so uncomplicated that we don't even know we're doing it, is to fashion something of an unspoken contract with him. It happens imperceptibly. The newly acquired disciplines and spiritual principles harden into the terms of a quiet bargain struck with God: our allegiance for his cooperation. We do this and God does that. In a crazy way, we try to swap services.

When Ted was watching his floral business flounder and struggling just to meet his bills, he sat in with a small group of Christians where someone shared how he "had put God to the test and look how God blessed." He found himself wanting to say, "So what do you do when you tithe and you work hard and you keep your priorities in order, and you are still losing money? If this works for everyone else, then why not me?"

"My wife and I kept asking ourselves where we went wrong," he says. "I mean, had God led us into this business or not? We could only conclude that he had, in spite of all that had happened. But I think that, in a good sense, this experience finally moved us out of the of-course-God-is-going-to-bless-me realm.''

It can be jolting when you first begin to realize that God does not offer guarantees; when you start to acknowledge the promises he never made.

Most of us don't really understand what "terms" we have placed in our contracts until, in one way or another, they aren't met. Often we never see what our false expectations were until they have not been fulfilled. It's the empty spaces, the ones we didn't even know were there, that begin to hurt.

It is easy, for instance, to feel that the safety and warmth of a Christian environment offers protection and immunity from the disappointments you would face outside it. One midwestern wife spoke of how she and her husband had finished seminary with another couple, close friends with whom they hoped to begin a church planting venture in the northwest.

"We were committed to the same philosophy and the same ideals, but much more than that, we were committed to each other as couples. We used to joke about how we would grow old together," she says.

They thought they understood each other's shortcomings, the scars they carried, their own peculiar vulnerabilities. The church began to grow and take off in a way that surpassed even their wildest expectations. In the process, one of the two couples began to make major shifts in their philosophy of leadership. There seemed to be no way to resolve their growing differences, and in order to preserve a single-minded approach, one couple had to leave and begin again, in another location.

How does this wife view her abrupt departure and the severing of such close relationships? "It sobered me up a ton," she explains. "I see how fragile we are as people, how much baggage we carry from our pasts. Before this, I always thought that, inside the body of Christ, God would somehow protect me from other people's failures." In other words, she became aware of her false expectation in hindsight, only when she realized it was not being met.

Many of us knew all along that pain and loss and struggle were just part of the human condition, as common to the Christian as to the man on the street. But somehow, the way it affected us would be different. Says one man who is now the wiser, "I really thought that what I *knew* about God—my notebooks full of information, my spiritual expertise—would protect me from feeling the full force of the things I dreaded the most, things like failure and rejection and inadequacy."

Another woman looks back on the years of infertility and four miscarriages that came in the process of trying to have children. "It wasn't the suffering in this regard that surprised me," she says. "But in my understanding of faith and the abundant life, rejoicing in the Lord and wading through grief were two incongruous concepts. I expected difficult circumstances, but I didn't expect to *feel* them emotionally in the same way any mother would. I thought somehow that God would let me live above the pain. But he didn't."

So it is that when we begin to release God from a contract he never signed, we take our first steps in learning, really learning, what it means to *trust* him. Years after our original introduction to Christ, many of us have entered, as new initiates, the real rigors of spiritual growth; the slowly spun, weathered variety that comes only when you have taken your tenth basic step to Christian maturity and fallen down.

The principal means of going forward, in a personal and spiritual sense, became what we least expected—disappointment. It is a discovery that, even now, seems strange, like being led home by going abroad.

CHAPTER 6

Rude Awakenings

Seeing the End of Your Own Innocence

I think I believed that my life was on moveable rollers, and if I tried hard enough, I could rearrange the pieces most any way I wanted.

Jay Larson, 34

———————◆———————

A s we move from our twenties through the decade of our thirties, many of our youthful illusions become exposed to the harsh rays of real life. Heroes come down off their pedestals, the new and exciting settles into routine, we get saddled with responsibilities and demands. Our life may be taking a very different course than the one we thought God had laid out for us. The passage from youth to the advanced youth of middle age opens up exciting possibilities, but it contains its own series of subtractions as well—reminders not only of what we are becoming, but of what we might have been.

Often in the process of that passage, something unexpected happens that has a way of dislodging some of our most valued dreams, throwing us off balance. I call that a rude awakening. It can take many forms—a death, an accident, a lost job, a broken relationship, an undesirable move, a dashed hope, a betrayal.[1] A rude awakening is closely akin to the term that Daniel Levinson, in his book about men's life stages, called a "culminating event," a circumstance that serves as a marker for the conclusion of young adulthood.[2]

A rude awakening, though, is not necessarily a monumental event. Other people might have negotiated the same turn in the road as though it were only a slight detour. But for the person who feels "rudely awakened," there is an inner sense of being stopped short, of wanting to ask, "Hey, what's going on here? My life is not unfolding the way I thought it would." It feels as though a stray chapter from someone else's life has been thrown right into the middle of your own.

STOPPED SHORT

It is strange how our lives as individuals can parallel the larger story of the times in which we have lived. One of the great figures of our generation's childhood was John F. Kennedy. His Boston accent charmed us. His regal, prince-like bearing made him an indelible hero, and Jackie in her pill box hat added the elegant touch.

The Kennedy years were what Theodore White called a "magic moment in history," when gallant men danced with beautiful women and great deeds were done, and the barbarians behind the gate were held back.[3] Even the later disclosures of Kennedy's less-than-noble tendency to court less-than-queenly women have not completely erased the aura of Camelot we associate with that time.

Those magic moments, and with them a national era, came to an abrupt end on a Dallas parkway in 1963. One moment this couple was waving to cheering crowds from the back seat of a black limousine; the next minute they were racing to a hospital. Jackie recounted that ride in utterly human terms: how she found herself struggling to put back the pieces of tissue that fell from the wound in her husband's head, as though the man in her lap was a doll that could be patched and fixed; as though the whole event could be backed up and rewound like a movie.

That picture of Jackie as the stunned widow, standing alone in her stiff pink coat, is a life-sized image of the sheer fragility of human experience. One minute life is moving ahead smoothly. The next minute it appears to stop and stand still.

Many of us have events, especially in our thirties, that though smaller in scale and of much less social consequence to be sure, markedly alter our direction or outlook. For some, they are climactic; for others, just epiphanal moments. But surprises, disappointments, and tragedies divide our experience into small before and after categories. The earth was made round, says one African proverb, so that we would not see too far down the road. Or as John Lennon is often quoted, "Life is what happens while you are busy making other plans."

As it does for most of us, such an experience began for me quite unexpectedly. About the time my children were all in school and I was ready to move out into some brand new ventures, I sat across the desk from a doctor who told me point blank, with all the solemn finality of a minister's benediction, that I did not have the flu. I was pregnant. The queen of infertility, and I was pregnant.

I could not believe my ears. I left his office in a daze, clutching my abdomen as though it had a mind of its own, and might suddenly decide to walk in the opposite direction. At home, the news of another baby was greeted with such excitement that I began to abandon my misgivings. "This is better than Christmas!" our daughter said, as she ran off to measure whether her old doll bed would hold a real baby.

The longer I thought about a third child, the more inviting the prospect became. This time I could relax and enjoy a baby. There were four people—not two—waiting for the arrival of this child who, as weeks turned into months, in my mind became more and more "the perfect child," the one with the even-tempered disposition, who would also read at two.

I had known nothing but uneventful pregnancies, and I didn't expect anything different this time. That was why I was doubly unprepared for that first wrenching pain and the sudden gush of blood that mark the threat of miscarriage. I was pushing a cart in a grocery store parking lot when it happened. I went home and went to bed.

For days on end, I laid in bed. I read books, stared out the window, and prayed, hoping fervently that this life would stay inside me. But somewhere in those hours, it dawned on me that I had no real control over whether I kept or lost this baby. For once, I had come up against something that I could not *will* to be different. I was powerless.

Strangely, my predicament brought to mind a game my son and I used to play when he was four years old and able to conjure up new worlds in his imagination with ease. First, he would gather the necessary articles of his life—his toy gun, his teddy bear, and a box of Cheez-Its—then he'd climb into a long clothes closet. After a while I'd hear him call, "Hey, Mom, come on in here with me."

"Why Brady? What do you want me in the closet for?" I'd answer.

"Because there are lions and tigers out there, Mom. And if you come in here with me, we can shoot them all —dead."

Having never been one to pass up truly important work, I would pile into his closet, find some less cluttered spot in a dark corner, and feed Cheez-Its to this young hunter as he fearlessly ridded the bedroom of wild beasts. Finally, we would emerge, the triumphant pair.

My current bedroom scene was totally unlike that. How I wished you could dispense with real threats that easily, that there was some human means of keeping the lions and tigers at bay.

But there was not. Within a few weeks, I delivered a little boy one morning in the doctor's office. All his parts were miniature, skillfully-crafted, doll-like, and just as still. The obstetrician held up his tiny form and offered his condolence. I felt pathetically unprepared to say good-bye to this child as he lay cold and quiet atop a doctor's cabinet.

A few months later, after we had begun to absorb this loss, I was at the hospital visiting a friend when, with no warning, I rounded the corner of the newborn nursery. Instantly I took a deep breath. Just the sight of those babies, their cheeks plump and pink with life, took me back. This was the way babies were supposed to look. I shrunk from the contrast between their soft faces and the memory of that gaunt little boy with his eyes sealed shut.

More than the isolated incident of this miscarriage, I began to sense how carefully carved in my mind—and how many—were the images of *how life ought to be.* Careers without glitches, fellowship with less friction, smart children who kept well-decorated rooms neat, and babies—especially babies—who nestled their pink cheeks in warm receiving blankets. I never knew I had such a scripted picture.

Somehow I sensed, as only a woman can, that I would not be able to have another child. I could hear the door creaking shut. The memory of this child was a wrenching exit to the child-bearing years, a rending of my neatly arranged cosmos, my own personal rude awakening.

That episode left me wondering what other stray calamities might come home to roost. I knew I was now officially outside the protective bubble I had been living in for years. I finally realized in a deep personal sense that my life was not a menu from which I was free to pick only the selections that suited my tastes.

SLOW DAWNINGS

Not everyone likens this maturing process to a rude awakening. For some, there is no calamitous event. One day folds into the next, one deadline after another is met, and there is little time to reflect. Instead of rude awakenings, there are slow dawnings. Little by little, you just sense your life evolving into something different than you imagined. Sometimes, a feeling of stagnation, disequilibrium, or mild depression sets in. The results of choices made earlier become plain, yet not easily reversed. Options for change seem to have narrowed, but responsibilities have grown.

Those slow dawnings usually take place in the decade of our thirties, when we face up to our own personal "nevers." I am never going to be head of the firm, or have children of my own, or be rich and famous. However that "never" may present itself, it slowly dawns on us that we've been chasing a carrot on a stick.

It can be a sobering realization when you see you may not be able to soar to the heights you thought. "I had always thought of myself as a person with well above-average abilities," says one woman, a middle-manager for a state agricultural agency. "But when I moved from Lincoln to Chicago I realized that there are a lot of talented people out there. I did well but others were doing better. I grew up expecting to be discovered down at the corner drugstore but more and more I suspect I will just plod along."

This woman's sentiments are echoed by many people in their thirties. This is often a time of introspection, of critical self-evaluation. Have I measured up? What would life be like now if I had made different choices earlier in my life? What changes can I make now? Those kinds of questions speak of lost opportunities and hidden regrets, but they are necessary and often lead to mid-point changes of direction or corrections.

The Illusion of Success

Even for those who have actually attained the goals they had in mind, there is often an unexpected let down. They've gotten what they thought they wanted, the fantasy gratified. The corner office. The book published. The brilliant baby. And it isn't enough—not for long. Something is still missing. The feeling of incompleteness stubbornly returns. Success is rarely 'all it's cracked up to be.

By the age of 35, Grant had reached his goal that had been ten years in the making, his fantasy gratified. He was finally able to open his own psychiatric practice on the outskirts of a large metropolitan city. This is what he'd gone to medical school for, the reason he'd paid his dues in someone else's clinic and moved his family half-way around the country.

For the first year or so he still felt charged whenever he drove up to the building with the name of his practice out front. He enjoyed hiring staff that he felt could give quality care. But, in fact, he had exchanged one set of problems for another. Some of the magical hopes he had attached to his dream evaporated in the never-ending string of "dailies." It wasn't as special as he thought.

A curious kind of flat, hollow feeling, like soda pop when all the fizz is gone, began to follow him, the question, *So what?* half-forming on his lips. Where was he supposed to go from here? What do you do for an encore at this point? It was hard to admit the disappointment— the strange sense of deflation he felt—not upon the loss of a dream, but on realizing it.

What Grant found—and what many of us discover upon realizing a dream—is the mirage-like quality of success. Euphoria is short-lived and not nearly as portable as we would like. Once we have struggled our way to the top of some mountain, another one appears that beckons us to climb again. There is always someone else who has done better, achieved more. One of the most ironic kinds of disappointment of all is the kind that comes when we realize that outward success rarely changes inner realities. We can't fill up the empty spaces within by achieving even our biggest dreams.

The Illusion of Control

Reckoning with old dreams forces us to face many of our false notions, one of which is the illusion that we are the master of our fate. This is the deceptive feeling that if we're smart, if we stay on our toes, life will work the way we've planned. If we just try hard enough, we can stay in control. Somehow by piety, planning, or flint-faced determination we can keep our world intact. The M & M's will melt in our mouths, as the package said, not in our hand.

Rude awakenings, or even slow dawnings, convince us, on an emotional level, of something we thought we knew all along: Sometimes there are forces at work much bigger than we are. We are not the master of our destiny. As one friend said of his current dilemma, "I realized there was no human way possible that I was going to worm my way out of this thing."

In April of Ted's first year in the floral supply business, his accountant called to congratulate him. The business was prospering under Ted's management. "Five years from now, you could own this firm outright," he said. "Keep up the good work."

One month later an employee filed suit against Ted for having let him go. The employee won. Within a week the manager for one of Ted's three divisions said she was leaving that day and going to work for a competitor. She took all her accounts with her. Then as though he had entered some Job-like progression, a string of customers went bankrupt on him—eight in one week.

Ted began to prepare for his July design show with more than usual energy. This once-a-year open house was the floral design school that Ted's business was known for all over town, the one-day affair that sparked his cash flow.

"Oh, God," Ted prayed, "if you could just let this open house do well."

But as Ted packed up the boxes from the sale that day, he didn't have to look at the computer printout to know the event had been less than a success. He would be fortunate to break even. "It was at that point," Ted says, "that I realized I had come into a situation that was beyond my control. Nothing I did was working. Not even prayer. I saw how easily this business could slip through my fingers and I felt helpless."

What Ted was expressing is the way it feels to be confronted with the limits of being human. The deceptive sense that we are in control of our own life fades, and what takes its place is the first stirrings of a healthy dependence on God and an appreciation of our need for other people.

The Illusion of Exemption

Another false conception is similar to the illusion that we can control our own lives. We grow up with the idea that pain and heartache, evil and death will remain outside the walls of our castle. Unexpected, unpleasant things happen to other people. But not us. Not now. And not this way.

Somewhere enroute to maturity, this illusion also starts to break down. We begin to personalize the theological reality of living in a renegade world. We realize our vulnerability. We start to understand that God never promised us immunity. Some of the effects of this fallen state of affairs are going to touch our lives too.

When Susan discovered she was developing some of the same arthritis that had plagued her mother all her life, she was frustrated and a bit scared. But she was not too upset. Everyone's life included some hardship, she reasoned.

When her marriage started to slip, though, that was another story. "I could not understand this transformation I saw taking place in Jim or the way our relationship was slowly degenerating before my eyes." She had been drawn to Jim's ability to think well and to put those ideas together in ways that other people could grasp easily. There was a verse in Daniel that had always reminded her of Jim, that, as was said of Daniel, "light and understanding and wisdom" dwelt in him.

That image became harder to reconcile with the man who also felt the need, on occasion, to go out and get good and drunk after a hard day in the ministry. Obviously, something was eating away at him. Eventually, he dropped out of seminary to go into business with his father.

"I remember one night," Susan recalls, "when we went out to dinner with some friends and Jim had too much to drink. He was right out there in the middle of the floor going crazy dancing and everyone was looking on and laughing. But I felt like the man before me was dying; he sure wasn't the guy from Daniel. It broke my heart to watch."

When Jim filed for divorce a year later, and Susan took the girls and moved back home to Oregon, she was feeling desperate. Her life was out of control. "I had never doubted that, as Christians, we wouldn't have our share of problems," she says. "But we wouldn't divorce. It wouldn't happen to me."

"I didn't think that this would happen to me." Or that it could happen to me. How many times have we all thought like that, if we were honest?

That's part of what makes the Bible such an inviting book; the book worth returning to when we experience the unexpected. Its comfort is found in its honesty. Even the way in which God orders the story contains a message. The Bible begins on a fundamentally positive note and ends in triumph, clean and sure; but in between Genesis and Revelation, there are adulterous kings and reluctant prophets, and at least one woman too impatient to sit still for long. It's real life, not fairy tales.

That's encouraging. We can open this book and find

our lives on its pages. This is the normal Christian life—
this one, with bills waiting to be paid and relationships
in need of repair. It's not immunity we've been given, it's
grace. What Christianity offers is not a detour around
trial and disillusionment but the courage to move
through them.

While our backgrounds may have left us with a different impression, God never promised any of his children
an escape hatch from pain. The rude awakenings and
slow dawnings that come with growing older invite us to
unpack the heavy suitcase we've carried, the one filled
with oversized dreams and false expectations. We need a
lighter load, less burdened by unrealistic goals and false
pictures of ourselves, of crazy notions about what this
life can deliver. It is an utterly necessary discarding process.

Because faith in an illusion is the shakiest kind.

A THRESHOLD TO THE FUTURE

When a person is in the midst of facing up to and letting
go of old dreams, it is often difficult to see beyond the
immediate struggle at hand. The temptation is to level
out in resignation, tune out, and get mired in disillusionment. Walter Lippman is famous for saying that while we
all grow older, it is by no means certain that we all grow
up. I think he meant that if we don't recognize the tran-
sitional passage we are in, we often stay stuck there.

But if we ride that process through, if we take hold of
our hopes and expectations and reel them in a bit, we
discover something unforeseen. *There is hidden wealth
in our disappointed dreams.* There is an "abundant life"
offered us; not the external, measurable, bigger and better kind we had envisioned, but it's there. We stand on
the threshold of discovering a deeper sense of personal
identity, renewed relationships, and a more realistic
faith. Our ideas about what constitutes the good life take

on a different shape. Our own small contribution to the world starts to seem big enough. A sense of renewal replaces the feeling of stagnation and decline.

This process in a person's life is one that starts on the inside and moves outward. Growing up—really growing up—means that we have to grapple with what's happening inside us, in our own private world of relationships and expectations. When that internal work takes place, the real changes begin.

Most of these benefits are best understood when they are observed in the lives of people who have wrestled with disappointed ideals. And so we begin to look at these same people's lives with more of a contemporary focus, exploring the way God has built and is building something better on top of the rubble of their crumbled dreams.

Part III

The Hidden Wealth in Disappointed Dreams

CHAPTER 7

Inner Spaces
The Search for Authenticity

I've bounced around for so many years as a mother, volunteer, school teacher, graduate student, and taxi driver that I no longer have much of an idea who I am.

Melinda Devoe, 40

───────────── ◆ ─────────────

When some significant aspect of a person's outer world is shaken, a quieter hidden process begins on the inside as well. Somewhere between the ages of thirty-five and forty-five, a shift in focus occurs and our attention is drawn more to our own internal dynamics. Often this is precipitated by a disappointment that jars our sense of identity, of who we are.

But whatever the reason, this shift in focus is a God-given opportunity to take personal inventory of our lives. It is not meant to be a cul-de-sac of self-absorption; rather it is a chance to reassess, to sink our personal roots down into what we are recognizing is really true about ourselves, our relationships, our faith, our lives. It is as though God knows we need the time to stand back and see ourselves from a larger perspective: What were our dreams, why were they so important to us as individuals, and where do we go from here? Sometimes that internal work takes the shape of a full-blown "identity crisis," a term that seems predictable and trendy until you find yourself in the middle of one.

The process of taking an inside look—an identity crisis —was, for me, the result of a dream that failed to materialize. In the mid-'80s my husband and I invested four years in launching a leadership institute at Glen Eyrie, the Colorado conference center for a Christian organization known as The Navigators. This work-study program attracted students from all over the U.S. and many other countries as well, and it consumed the energies of five staff couples who gave their full-time attention to this effort. We worked to provide the opportunity for intense spiritual and personal help in a warm environment, at a fraction of the cost of a traditional seminary experience. It was a good dream. But after four years we were forced to admit that it was not financially feasible to continue the program as it was constructed.

Those four years required a heavy personal investment on my part. Consequently, the change in plans deeply affected me. I found that when I could no longer hold onto the idealized image of myself as one half of this dynamic couple in ministry, when the role I had been comfortable with was no longer appropriate, I began to flounder. Who was I, then? I didn't know. For a while, I felt like I had lost myself—a classic characteristic of an identity crisis. I came to associate those years with a word I loathed, failure. Although some wonderful things came from that time, we had not been able to accomplish the goals we had set. And failure was another thing that, without having realized it, I believed that trusting God would save me *from.*

The decade of our thirties (and sometimes up until the age of forty-five) is notorious for such inner wrestlings. This is the time when slightly balding men buy little red sports cars and mothers of small children feel the overpowering desire to have Ph.D.s attached to their names. This is when internal voices arise, posed as questions: What pushes me so hard? Why am I doing this day after day? Is it worth it? Why do I feel so alone in it all? These are but a sampling of the questions raised. Discovering the answers is a process that takes us on something of an inner journey.

A SEARCH FOR AUTHENTICITY

Perhaps this process can best be described as a search for authenticity, for an identity that exists apart from all that we have accomplished or any of the roles we play.

This search for genuine identity is what Gerald May, the author of *Addiction and Grace,* calls an "underlying constancy of self." He says that what we long to experience is "some foundation of self that is invulnerable to any other experience, unaffected by anything else that might happen to us."[1] This search, he says, is one that brings us closer to the center of what the Old Testament calls our *heart.* It is our real self, a sense of inner home, the place where we experience the closest, most directly feeling contact with the presence of God.

In some ways we have been on this kind of identity search all our lives. Underneath the veneer, the faint little question always flickers: "Who am I, really?" I am someone's wife, someone's mother, someone's teacher, someone's daughter—that much I know. But apart from what I can do, separate from the ways that others see me, who am I? It is almost like asking, once I get past my string of achievements and demands, past all the roles I play, *is there anyone home?*

Actually, this kind of identity search is an old-as-Adam, universal quest. You can hear it in the way Tolstoy likened one part of his own journey: "I felt that something had broken within me on which my life had always rested, that I had nothing left to hold on to. . . ."[2] He is speaking of that floundering sense of emptiness that comes when some of the ways you've always used to define yourself no longer apply. Robert Frost talked of how his life had been a progression in which *he lost enough to find himself.*

For those of us in the postwar generation, our search for authenticity is expressed in more contemporary terms. However it surfaces, though, the drive for a genuine sense of individuality has always been a powerful one for us.

A middle-aged father of three talks about how he knows who he is on paper and plastic. He only has to look in his wallet. There he finds his social security number, his company I.D., pictures of his children, and an array of credit cards. And then, he says half-jokingly, "Some days I wonder if I lost my credentials, could I prove that I exist?"

For Grant, this quest became apparent when, somewhere in his thirties, he found himself missing his father, though the man had been dead for ten years. The relentless pressure of his life, the demands from all quarters, made him wish his father was still alive. He felt he needed someone to lean on for support. The load he was asked to shoulder as a husband, father, and employer left him longing to know his father as someone who could point the way.

"When I look back on our relationship now," Grant says, "I realize that there wasn't much friction between us. Mostly we just frittered away the time being cordial. Now, at this point in my life, I realize that coming to terms with myself as a man is directly related to the support and connection I should have experienced with the most significant man in my life—my father. Part of who I am is linked to who I was, and am, as this man's son."

Whenever we begin to ask questions about personal identity, we enter spiritual domain. We can see the answers reflected, in a biblical sense, in the way that Jesus dealt with individuals. He looked behind Peter's 'Simon facade,' and told him that one day soon, his identity as a stable, rock-like man (Cephas) would come to the fore.[3] Jesus reminded another of his disciples, Nathaniel, that he knew him before they had ever met.[4] Nathaniel's innermost identity was held securely in the mind and heart of God.

So there is nothing essentially new or unusual about coming to a point in life where your focus shifts internally. An identity crisis, a search for authenticity, is primarily fueled by any or all of three factors: the simple process of growing older, shifting self-images, or disappointment in others. All of these are especially common to the era known as *midlife.*

GROWING OLDER

Just the ordinary process of aging tends to strip us, to pare us down, to challenge our notions about ourselves. We are no longer the bright, young whiz-kids with all the fresh ideas. We are beginning to slow down some. Maybe the career that required so much time has already peaked and begun to recede as noticeably as a hairline.

Our children grow up before our eyes, the laugh lines around our eyes turn into honest wrinkles, and it gets harder and harder to hold on to the illusion of being forever young. We aren't ready to party at 12 a.m., we're already asleep. Columnist Dave Barry insists that one of the most traumatic aspects of turning forty is realizing that we no longer have the same body we had when we were twenty-one. "I know I don't," he writes. "Sometimes when I take a shower I look down at my body and I want to scream: "Hey, THIS isn't my body! THIS body belongs to Willard Scott!"[5]

New bulges appear on our bodies in strange places, and as Judith Viorst says in her book *Necessary Losses,* we start "to inspire far less lust than we do respect. We're not quite prepared to settle for only respect."[6] She quotes from a wistful poem entitled "The Age of Maturity":

When I was young and miserable and pretty
And poor, I'd wish
What all girls wish: to have a husband,
A house and children. Now that I'm old, my wish
Is womanish:
That the boy putting groceries in my car
See me. It bewilders me that he doesn't see me.[7]

A future of endless possibilities no longer strings before us. Time starts to be measured in terms of "how
many years do I have left?" rather than just chronologi-
cal age. The simple process of aging breaks down some of
our cherished images of self and challenges us to reach
for a deeper, more intransigent sense of identity. We are
forced to reach behind appearances and address the question of substance. This is our chance to begin to offer
others the whole of who we are and in that offering, to
discover a deeper level of personal authenticity.

SHIFTING IMAGES OF SELF

The changes in youthful appearance and capacities, however, are not the only ones that force us to reevaluate.
Our self-perception shifts in other ways as well, from an
idealized image of ourselves to a more accurate, balanced
understanding.

Most of us spend the greatest portion of our lives fash-
ioning an idealized image of ourselves—some version of a
competent, pleasing personality that we feel comfortable
in presenting to an onlooking world. Early in life we
learn how to fine tune our talents and how to offer what
is required of us in order to be valued by others. We
become heavily invested in our titles and advanced de-
grees, our individual expertise, and sharp presentations.
Our strengths we know how to highlight; our weaknesses
we have learned to hide. And in a convoluted way, our

hope is that God is just as committed as we are to keeping that idealized image intact.

The fear of exposure keeps this fragile false identity stuck firmly in place. We are afraid that someone might take a peek behind that mask and discover an ordinary little boy or girl, unsure and a bit overwhelmed with life, convinced that the only thing that makes them worthwhile is the abilities others find useful or commendable. "The fact that I could sing well enough to entertain or inspire people," one friend explained in her own metaphorical way, "became something of a screen I hid behind. It was like a coat two sizes too big that I hoped no one would peek through and laugh."

We learn how to play it safe; how to keep our real feelings, needs, and vulnerabilities so protected from sight, that as the years go by, our real self is almost totally hidden. We become plastic people, not the fully human, wonderfully alive people God meant us to be, but experts in pretending—strangers, even to ourselves.

Fortunate are those for whom some setback or new development challenges that idealized self-image. That is part of what Ted experienced when his business slid into deep financial strain. He had always been the kind of guy that others looked to for advice. He stood out in a crowd as a natural leader, a model of integrity and good business sense. He was the one always asked to give workshops or gather a men's group for weekly breakfasts.

"I had built my life around my idea of what an accomplished Christian businessman looked like," Ted says. "This was the image I groomed myself for, the person I felt God intended me to be."

But when his floral business hit serious financial difficulties, when survival became the issue, Ted began to take a back seat. People were not looking to him for much of anything. For the first time, he was in a men's group of all business owners, and he didn't lead the group. He said very little. He felt he had nothing to share.

The group was led by a younger man, a new Christian for whom everything was going beautifully. "This guy would make a move," Ted recalls, "and God would bless him hand over fist. He came out of his contract negotiations with stuff I never heard of." It was hard to watch others do so well without concluding that all his problems were a commentary on his own failures.

Ted had always prided himself on being able to meet his financial obligations as they arose. "I think my lowest point," he says, "was when I had to call a Jewish supplier who knew I was a practicing Christian and ask him to help us work out our payments on time. Later, as I realized how many people who owed me money refused to even return my phone calls, I saw that my candidness was more of an opportunity to show some character than I thought."

At the time, though, Ted felt humbled to the core. Struggling with his business had a way of stripping away everything he thought he had—his abilities and strengths, his concept of himself as the young, successful go-getter.

Though it felt like his outer skin was being peeled away and he fought the urge to cover up the pain, Ted recognizes that this dismantling process left him in a better position than he realized. "I became a lot more honest about myself," Ted says. "It's hard to hide your weakness and your pain when you are stretched to your limits like that. I feel like I emerged as more of a whole person —a human being, rather than a performing artist. What I have to give people now, who I am, flows as much from my failures as it ever did from my success."

When we are forced to reach beneath our idealized image of ourselves, we discover that there is an average, ordinary person there; one with needs and feelings, with particular opinions and longings. Beneath our polished appearance exists a real person who was embraced at the cross, a son or daughter of God with an innate identity that can't be earned, only claimed. A. W. Tozer once said that because God thundered from the heavens, "I AM," on this basis we are enabled to answer back in feeble, but authentic voices, "*I am, too.*" There really is someone home.

DISAPPOINTMENT IN OTHERS

Our lives are lived in the context of relationships with other people—friends and mentors, spouses and parents—and invariably, we have invested much of who we are in our trust and dependence on them. When they fail us in some way, the way we view ourselves is often deeply shaken.

As a generation, we have never been in short supply of heroes. We have a long history of attaching our personal hopes and dreams to mythic figures like Martin Luther King, Jr. or Robert Kennedy. Looking up to people, believing what they said was what they meant, came naturally to us for the longest time. When that faith was broken, through death—as in King and Kennedy's case—or through the discovery that many of our heroes had feet of clay, disillusionment set in. Our dreams and the picture of where we fit into them had to be reevaluated.

A similar process takes place in the arena of close relationships, only the disappointment when someone close leaves you hanging high and dry is much more profound. One import-export entrepreneur I spoke with, a man in his late thirties, shared with me that his biggest disappointment as he had gotten older centered around a mentoring relationship with a man in his church. "This guy led me to Christ in his youth group," he says, "and over the years he became a kind of father figure to me, a man of integrity I could take my cues from."

My friend watched this man's influence in the business world grow to national and international stature, and slowly, he began to follow in similar steps. "That's why I found it a bit ironic," he relates, "to have been on an overseas trip when I heard that this man had been having an affair with a woman in the church. I felt let down, as though maybe this man's failure had invalidated a lot of my own life as well as his. I remember turning to my wife and telling her that somehow it all made my own achievements seem a bit stale. It stole some of the joy."

What my friend was voicing that day is a disappointment born of the fear of being left on your own. Suddenly the hero spot is empty. A parent has died, or is starting to lapse into second childhood, and is not there to be leaned on. Instead, they're leaning on you. Or our parents don't retire to Florida the way they're supposed to; they divorce and flounder solo. Or the friend you so admired seems to turn on you. Somehow, it feels as though there is no one *out front* and yet, there may not be enough support *around* you and you are forced, finally, to learn what it means to gather strength from *inside.* You begin to reach for your own separate identity, the part of you that is not fused with the success or failure, the faithfulness or unfaithfulness, of anyone around you.

Letting go of some of our deeper dependencies can be painful because they protect us from that raw sense of feeling alone. And *alone* can be an awful way to feel. As long as I can idealize someone by lionizing his strengths and overlooking his humanness, then I never have to face the need to find my own rightful strength. I can depend on someone else. To face someone else's limitations is also to admit my own—and to be left feeling alone and dependent on God in a whole new way.

I think of how I usually prefer to ride the waves when we are at the ocean with our children. I rarely choose to face such big, unknown waters without first grabbing one of the kids' rafts. The ocean is still a strange place to a woman who's more at home in the mountains. You never know what creatures lurk beneath all that foam and spray. And in some childish part of my brain, I still think that the crabs won't bite my toes and the jellyfish won't sting me—as long as I'm holding on to that raft. Pure illusion, I know. But I find it as hard to walk into the ocean standing on my own two feet as I do to move forward in life without leaning on another person to keep me safe.

The closer the bond between two people, the harder the blow when that someone deserts or disappoints us, and the more we struggle with questions about our own identity. Susan remembers her sense of grief as she watched the image of the man she thought was Jim begin to unravel. "I knew this guy had so much to offer, an intensity and strength I found hard to describe," she says. "But there was a darker side, too, with wild mood swings and unpredictable anger. That was the part I had never let myself admit, until it was too late."

It took Jim's leaving to bring Susan to the point where she started to ask some of the personal questions she should have asked much earlier. For the longest time after he left she was numb, vacant, unconnected. Then she began to feel like she'd been robbed. She says, "I realized that I had only given Jim the parts of myself that I felt he wanted. He had taken that, but somehow I always knew that I never satisfied him."

She had done whatever it took to please this man, doling herself out in little bits until it seemed that there was nothing left. She felt "invisible" to herself. People would ask her what she wanted to do now. Where did she want to go from here? Susan had no idea.

"It was then," she says, "that I saw I had lived like a chameleon all my life. It wasn't just with Jim. I had been a blank mirror that reflected whatever color or shape was put before it. When Jim was no longer there to lean on, I was forced to discover who was the 'I' that had been absorbed by the 'we.' "

So it is for all of us that once our bubbles begin to burst, our trusted notions about our selves and those we love start to fade, and we begin to take a deeper look at who we really are. This journey is a rite of passage in the mysterious thing called "growing up."

It is a new beginning in a personal and spiritual sense —a fresh start at taking the small, wobbly steps of learning what it means to stand on your own two feet.

CHAPTER 8

Becoming Real
Growing Up From the Inside Out

I got tired of imitation margarine and fake fur. I got tired of synthetic fabric and man-made snow and wearing a toupee. But most of all, I got tired of an imitation me.

Ronald Castle, 36

◆

When the actress Glenn Close was given an honorary degree by her alma mater, The College of William and Mary, she was also asked to give the commencement address in place of George Bush who politely declined.

She admits that for a long time she had no idea what she would say when it came time to speak. She had only been asked to do this in the first place, she realized, because as an actress, she had excelled at the difficult art of pretending to be someone else, to say someone else's lines.

She could think of each of the characters she had played and immediately, the words they would have said would form on her lips. She knew which would have shown herself politically astute and well-informed, which would never have been asked, and which would have declined as quickly as she received the invitation.

"But who am I? And what can I say?" she asked herself.

Despite her self-doubt, she went on to give a superb commencement address filled with the insight she had gained from her childhood, in the theatre, and from the support of various friends and mentors. If you read her speech, you realize that she had in her own mind and heart the words she needed to offer all along.

What Glenn Close mirrored that day, as she gave a commencement address where she played herself, was the developmental challenge we all face. At some point we must learn what it means *to speak our own lines.* The process of growing older, of facing the disappointments that jar our sense of identity, is one of discovering the role *we* are called to play, and gathering the courage to let go of the masks we have hidden behind. We begin to play our own parts and to own our own life.

We are not alone in facing this challenge. The whole question of individuality, of personal authenticity, is at the heart of what it means to follow Jesus. Here was a man who resisted the temptation to be anyone other than who he truly was, the Son of God. He refused to be made into a political reformer or a leader of the Jewish liberation from Rome, to grasp any other than his true identity as the Messiah. So when we set out to follow him, we embrace one who is committed to bringing us into a life built on honesty and lack of pretense, where what we experience is an ever-increasing freedom to be the person God had in mind when he created us.

We need to be aware, however, that this process contains no basic steps that, once followed, insure a sense of mastery and performance. There is no "how-to" formula that brings us into a solid sense of personal identity. That is why the process is best likened to an inner journey, one that is individualized and unpredictable, and over which we have little control. There are no short cuts to avoid the confusion and emptiness. Instead, the route wanders and meanders and only reveals how far you've come in a few scenic spots.

This process includes integrating the past and the present with new possibilities for the future, embracing once again the lost, abandoned parts of ourselves we have orphaned along the way. Perhaps somewhere back there, without realizing it, we turned our back on the person we wanted to be all along.

"I hate to admit that I am thirty-eight years old and only now beginning to realize that my goals were never *my* goals." So begins a man who spent years in the career field he was "expected" to enter and now, finally, is half way through a graduate program that will prepare him to teach. "Sometimes I get angry," he says, "that I have spent so many years on automatic pilot, headed toward the idea of being this great businessman, only to discover that was never me, really."

He grew up with tunnel vision for that goal, just doodling around in school, convinced that one day he would take over his father's manufacturing franchise. The business had consumed his father's energy and his son grew up never questioning that he would someday follow in his father's steps.

Now, with a kind of better-late-than-never attitude, he is starting to unplug from that goal. "I tried so hard to fit for so long, to be interested in the things that businessmen are interested in. Now that I'm away from that world I find I don't even look at the business section in the newspaper," he says.

Instead, he finds he really enjoys academic life, that the inquisitive world of the college professor is a much closer match to his own reflective nature. "I wish I had understood more of who I was when I was twenty-five, but I didn't," he adds. "I'm just thankful to be coming into my own now. I think I might have gone on forever just trying to be my father's son, never having lived my own life."

Twenty years ago Bob Dylan sang, "Something is happening in there, Mr. Jones." But Mr. Jones didn't know what it was. For the person willing to wade through the struggles of letting go of old dreams, willing to take an inside look, the process starts to look more like an inviting opportunity. He begins to sense that "Yeah, there is something happening in here. And it's starting to feel pretty good.''

When you're in the middle of this journey, it is natural to ask where it all leads. What comes to the person willing to tramp around in the backwoods of this kind of self-questioning? Some very encouraging things, it turns out. There is a hidden fortune in disappointment when it forces you to take a closer look at who you are.

THE FREEDOM TO LIVE WITHIN YOUR LIMITS

One of the most recognizable changes that emerges is a new ability to live inside your own human limitations. Some of the pressure to be good at everything—to be *omnicompetent*—is replaced by the quieter contentment of offering your own particular contribution. Many describe it as a new inner freedom—a release from the life-long urge to please, to fill in the gaps of everyone else's expectations for their lives.

This is no small feat, though, particularly for our generation. Our congenital weakness for great expectations and big dreams is that much of those demands became focused squarely on our *selves*. We were the ones who were supposed to cure cancer within our lifetime and write an end to poverty. We are the first to attempt the amazing task of trying to be two sexes at once. No one who had braces and their college education paid for should be merely average, right?

Just the sheer pace of life pushes us to adopt a super-human capacity. We race out the door to work in the morning, driven men and harried women with hurried children. Many hours later, with only a quick Clark Kent change of costumes, we become a homework supervisor or the congenial host or the innovative lover or some combination of all three, until we collapse for the night, wearied and worn—ready to get up and do it all over again tomorrow.

Is it any wonder that we feel pressure, the great, pounding internal pressure, to be more than who we are? Or something different from what we are?

Christians are in an even more demanding situation. Our expectations are often a cross between John Wayne and the Apostle Paul. The spiritual rationale of omnicompetence goes something like this: "The same God who created microscopic amoebas and flung the stars into space, also lives in me. I can, therefore, do whatever needs to be done. If I exercise enough faith and willpower, God will enable me to meet whatever needs arise." When we embrace this illusion, though, his voice is mistaken for another one among many, all pushing us to over-do, to live beyond our limits.

One businessman who lives in the glitzy hyperbole of Dallas spoke of how he learned, the hard way, that he was not superhuman. "I had lived for years," he says, "feeling like Atlas trying to hold up the world on my shoulders. Being a Christian somehow got all mixed up with that, and before long, I simply added a horde of Christian activities to the load I was already carrying."

He began to meet with a group of men on Saturday mornings for study and encouragement, only to find himself being nibbled away by envy. After all, this was Dallas. "I got tired of parking my decrepit Volkswagon behind those guys' BMWs," he says, "so I just made up my mind to double my efforts at work." He also became an elder in his church and led what seemed like a million men's groups, all the while straining to be a model husband and father.

Eventually, he also developed a bleeding ulcer. Four days in the hospital and a month's forced rest gave him some perspective. What he realized is what many of us discern when we finally reach midlife's burial ground and see for ourselves the grave markers of our impossible personal expectations.

"I came to grips with the fact that I was only good at a few things, really," he says. "Some guys are always going to have more than I do and that's O.K. The spiritual life is not a one man show. God has put me on a team." He sees himself as a Barnabas who affirms other people's contributions, while specializing in what he's really good at —relating to non-Christians. He became better able to say, "That's enough and that's O.K."

That's Enough and That's O.K.

What magical words of freedom those are. There is an inner release that comes when we begin to let go of some of those inflated illusions of ourselves. Like this Dallas businessman, we can major on a few things that grow out of the center of who we are and let the superfluous go. That requires the courage to say "no" more often, to let go of the all purpose call-me-for-anything role so easily played. Our sanity is restored to the measure that we discover our niche and capitalize on that.

Living with your limits, being able to say "that's enough and that's O.K." does require faith, but faith of a whole different sort. When we begin to recognize our gifts and inherent temperament, our best sphere of influence, we are, in fact, exercising faith in the thoughtful pattern in which God made each individual. We contribute to the whole as specialists in only a few things, learning to live in the humility of our God-given limitations.

"For years, I was shooting for a composite ideal which was really the best traits of two or three people I admired all rolled into one," explains a thirty-eight-year-old woman. "I just kept plugging along toward that goal, working to shore up my weak points, hoping to emerge as the phantom woman." When she finally realized, in her late thirties, that she wasn't reaching her goal, she began to take a closer look at her own identity. "I finally realized that I have an inherent set of abilities and interests, and that I can only be what I am." The faith she exercises now is the faith to become fully who she is, the woman God made her to be. She is finally able to say "that's enough and that's O.K." and mean it.

Accepting Those Limitations

When we begin to exercise that kind of faith, though, there are implications. Another aspect of living within your limitations is accepting how high, or how far, those limitations can take you. People who experience the freedom to be themselves are people who have brought their dreams into line with reality and feel at home there.

Sometimes the process of lowering your sights can be painful, as one woman who had invested years in the dream of being a well-known writer feels. For a long time it looked as though she might realize her best hopes. She had finished the largest part of four books in record time and appeared on a national television program that the producer called "a perfect show."

Then in the course of ghost-writing a book for a pair of husband-wife concert pianists, she happened to visit them in their home. "All of a sudden, I realized what real success in a professional field looked like," she says. "I listened to their phone ring at all hours for bookings. I watched their video and I saw firsthand the kind of promotional backing a publisher was willing to give their book."

With a jolt of insight, she knew that anything she had done was small potatoes in comparison. She wasn't ever going to be a "star"; she was simply a good utility writer who could capture someone else's story on paper. That was as far as her talent and life circumstances would take her.

For a while she floundered, feeling like the train had left without her. She was back at the depot in a small Midwestern town, with a husband who sold insurance and two kids who needed a ride to swim practice. "Well, all right," she said, "I guess this is it." Then, slowly, she took a fresh look at what "it" was. She began to reforge with her husband some of the connections they had lost in the time she had been buried at a computer. She carved out the space to breathe, to ride bikes with the kids, to read more books for pleasure.

"Once I stopped pushing to achieve the impossible," she says, "then my efforts weren't so weighted with the need to prove myself. Writing is much more enjoyable when you don't have to become the star of stage and screen or change western civilization in the process. I was free to enjoy the rippling effect of the impact I was having." She could walk in a bookstore and see the book she had written for someone else and think, "Hundreds of people will read these words and it's O.K. that my name isn't plastered on the pages. I found that I could have more, if I was willing to settle for a little less."

A NEW CAPACITY FOR INTIMACY

Another benefit of facing identity questions head-on is a deeper ability to love others. The reason is this: When we are uncomfortable with who we are, when our emotional survival depends on keeping our idealized image intact, we are not free to love. Our real energies are siphoned off in the task of protecting that image. We peek around at each other from behind a thousand masks, trying to escape the riskiness of letting someone into the inner circle of our lives.[1]

When we're afraid to let someone come close, afraid that they would leave if they saw our life was less-than-perfect, then the only emotional choice is to distance ourself from everyone who appears to have the power to cut us down to size. The prospect of intimacy feels like a dance in the dark, full of awkward little moments trying to avoid the pain of having one's toes stepped on.

Everything becomes tighter, more rigid and constricting, brittle to the emotional touch. We are cut off from experiencing what we were made for, that is, to love well and to be loved in return.

God created us with a longing for intimacy that no amount of super-achieving can satisfy. The more we come to peace with ourselves as God made us, the freer we are to enjoy the intimacy for which we were made. The energy used in the past to live defensively becomes channeled, instead, into someone else's life. We are no longer running scared, afraid of being exposed in the painful way we have worked so hard to avoid.

When life provides us the chance to come to terms with ourselves, when some stray calamity jolts us enough to make us drop our masks, a whole new world of relationships becomes possible. That's why a true inner journey always comes full circle. An inner journey includes outward movement as well.

This is why Ted, in some ways, views his business difficulties as a strangely liberating experience. It challenged his perceptions of himself and made him much freer to enjoy relationships. The overwhelming nature of his financial problems forced him to admit he was not in control. For once, he was the one who needed advice and consolation. "I began to discover that when I was with a friend," he says, "I was no longer working double-time trying to keep up my great image. It suddenly seemed pointless not to share with him the reality of what I was up against." A healthy sense of reciprocity, of mutual give-and-take, began to characterize some of his closer friendships.

"As a result of that time I see more of what it means to be totally present with someone," Ted says. "I can enjoy them with a kind of self-forgetfulness that comes from not having to defend myself or my ideas. I can hear what they are saying to me without getting my hackles up, and I can offer them the same honest ear." There is an inner ease that seeps into our relationships when we are not living in a state of vigilance, forever on guard to protect a fragile inner ego.

AN INNER RESILIENCE

While the questions that concern our identity foster inner freedom and a greater capacity for intimacy, there is a benefit even more fundamental. We begin to discover an inner resilience we did not know we possessed.

As long as we can keep our life moving forward the way we hoped it would, we never have to confront our own fears. Paradoxically, this only allows the anxiety to grow. If life never delivers us a blow so sharp we are knocked off our feet, we never know if we will be made strong enough to get up again. There is no way to grow strong in the broken places, as Hemingway wrote, no way to sense God meeting us at our point of need. We never get the chance to face some of our fears head-on and stare them down.

In Susan's life, she describes this process as "confronting the boogeyman." Being left alone in the role of a single parent was, for her, such an undesirable prospect that she never let herself consider the possibility—until she had to. And while she would never have chosen this situation, she nevertheless feels the bittersweet satisfaction of having confronted her worst fears and survived.

"I feel like someone who lived through a terrible automobile crash. I not only made it; in some important ways, I overcame," she says. As a result, she finds that she no longer rides as tight, braced for some imaginary disaster to come crashing down on her head, afraid that she will be swept away by something too devastating to handle.

There is enormous pleasure in touching bottom and finding it more solid than you thought. Ted sees some of the hidden success in his business struggles: "Sometimes

I feel like the Velveteen Rabbit. The difference in me now and five years ago is that I've had just enough of the threads rubbed bare and the seams stretched out of shape to know I'm real." He has experienced the satisfaction in character change. "I know what it is to survive and even profit by a situation that I thought for sure would do me in."

This inner resilience, so evidenced in Susan and Ted's lives, is the result of laying hold—in an emotional, experiential way—of a sense of the invincibility of your soul. Here beneath your fears is your most essential self, the innermost identity that the apostle Peter declared was "protected by the power of God" from now through all eternity.[2] This is your soul, your identity which required the death of Jesus to secure. No matter what adversity you encounter, you stand fundamentally protected because God has pledged himself to your preservation. The dismantling of your ego's superstructure brings you to the indestructible essence of your own soul.

Disappointment also offers the potential for inner wholeness. Our emotions have the opportunity to integrate with our mind. One man from the midwest, whose divorce had shattered his world, related how the experience opened up the whole emotional side of life for him. "I grew up on a farm," he explains, "where work and production were the big deals. As kids, we raised 4-H calves—slept with them and played with them—but when the fair came you hoped they won the blue ribbon because then you'd get a dollar a pound for the meat instead of 10 cents. Things lived and died and you learned to grow callous to the process. That was just life. You didn't waste time on feeling anything."

A few years after his own divorce, though, a friend pointed out to him that he was bitter, angry, even grief-stricken. How could that be? He didn't see himself that way. He didn't even have a frame of reference for any of those emotions. He knew that God promised to bind up the broken-hearted and to heal a wounded spirit, but it took him a long time to see that he fit in those categories. "I began to realize that you have to know that you're broken-hearted before you can experience any healing. Allowing yourself to feel, as well as to think and choose, is part of becoming a whole person."

Part of that inner resilience comes from the satisfaction of recognizing that pain and loss are intractable parts of life. It means that you don't have to spend enormous amounts of energy trying to avoid the unavoidable. In the process of disappointment you acquire the tools to deal with losses. You can feel the pain, and when the time comes, you can leave it behind and go on. You can live on the dark and the light side of life and gather the richness from both. You experience wholeness.

Without failure or disappointment, we would find some way to avoid facing our own neediness, and God would remain only a distant acquaintance. But having confronted that inner emptiness, every loss or disappointment becomes a hollow spot, a room in our own inn where God is invited, once again, to be at home. This is how our disappointments actually service our faith— these are the places where we sense God stirring in the deeply personal issues of our lives.

I find myself thinking how like Dorothy in the Wizard of Oz we are. We set off on the impossible journey of returning to where we belong, to our inner roots in Kansas. Somewhere en route, in the strangest places, we discover our own heart and mind and courage. Like Dorothy in her ruby red slippers, we find we have been given, in a deep spiritual sense, what we needed all along to make this trip. It is ourselves we uncover, the indestructible part of our soul held securely in the mind and heart of God.

That is part of the mystery, I think, in discovering more of who you are. At the same time that you are coming home to yourself, you are coming home to God. It's not simply that the porch light of your life has been left on to disguise a dark, vacant house.

There really is someone home.

CHAPTER 9

Loose Connections

Intimacy at the Crossroads

I can program a computer and design an auditing system for my company's accounts. I can cook a mean plate of Italian pasta. I even bake my own bread. But I don't do **relationships** *very well at all.*

Mary Whittaker, 34

———————◆———————

"Love is all we need," sang Mel Carter in 1966, and we sang along with him. If love was what was needed to make a relationship work, we thought we had enough to go around. We were the generation for whom equality and honest communication and getting-in-touch-with-your-feelings were supposed to break down the barriers to creating truly optimum relationships.

Unlike our parents who managed to place a man on the moon, we turned to conquer a different geography altogether; perhaps one that was even harder. We set out to shorten the distance between each other.

Close friendships, transparent relationships, deep conversation, honest sharing. We have sifted through a wide variety of phrases that all speak of the same goal—intimacy. Over the years we have cohabited and interfaced, committed too seldomly or loved too much, and now, who could draw a clear picture of "the perfect relationship?"

It all looked so easy in the beginning. If we could focus national attention on an unpopular war and racial equality, then establishing close connections between each other should be a simple task. We thought we had relationships all figured out. Then we actually got into one.

The relationship that naturally held the focus of our greatest expectations was, of course, marriage. Here in this liaison between a man and a woman countless dreams and plans and prayers have been centered. What more obvious place to hope for intimacy than between two people who have promised to share heart and soul, bed and bank accounts for a lifetime? And what more difficult?

In this most intimate of connections, the riddle of the gulfs between individuals can be clearly seen. At times they are small, like the space between two hands held in a lovers' stroll on a deserted beach. At other points, you could leap across a canyon easier than you could walk across a room and gather that familiar form in your arms.

Our generation has tried hard to improve on our parents' notion of husband and wife, marriage and family. "Married partners once settled for duty, but today's mates expect to be ecstatic lovers, intellectual colleagues, and partners in tennis and water sports," says Professor of Psychology Martin Seligman. "We even expect our partners to be loving parents, a historical peculiarity to anyone versed in the Victorian child-rearing model."[1]

Many of us saw our parents divorce or separate or just stand there paralyzed, unable to move toward each other in any meaningful way. Our generation hoped to do better. Here too, in the arena of relationships, we often wedded our expectations to our faith. "I thought that because my wife and I were two committed Christians and felt God had his hand in our relationship," explains a telephone salesman from Houston, "ours would start out like we'd been married for forty years. It would be a little slice of heaven on earth, and it wouldn't even *resemble* what my parents had." He is quick to admit, however, that though Christian principles have come to their aid, he and his wife have faced impasses they never thought they would.

HARDER THAN WE THOUGHT

So this thing of creating relationships that thrive, rather than merely endure, for a lifetime has been harder than we thought. Love may have been all we needed, but sometimes, love can be pretty hard to come by. A couple who began by feeling they owed each other "the sunshine in the morning" can feel years later that they are just passing each other in the dark. By the time they pay the mortgage, educate their children, and coach Little League, there is often little time for each other.

One reason we find the task of creating intimacy such a challenge is that we bring so much baggage from our checkered pasts into our present relationships. "I have to admit that I was dismayed to see what was really required to make a relationship work," says a man approaching forty and looking back over fifteen years of marriage. He grew up in a series of three homes with a mother who kept moving on to the next husband. "Throughout my thirties I always had the feeling that I would stick with my wife until I found this phantom woman who could give me the life I wanted," he says. "I didn't know what that was, but it was symbolized by that woman out there, somewhere." Though he didn't leave his wife, the anger and restlessness still took a toll on their marriage. Not until he saw that he could not use his present relationship to make up for the deficit of the past was he able to begin to establish a solid basis for intimacy with his wife.

Building genuine intimacy in a relationship is no simple task, even when a person knows, essentially, how to do that. As a psychiatrist, Grant spends the best part of his day wading in and out of people problems—especially breakdowns in relationships. And although he can offer his advice and counsel all day long, he finds it is another thing entirely to create the needed dynamics inside the context of his own marriage.

Only recently has he begun to see that the emotional detachment so necessary for his work environment is a detriment at home. There it easily becomes a protective front that even his wife cannot get through. He realizes that her depression is not totally the result of a difficult pregnancy and childbirth. It has something to do with her past—and with him.

"I've begun to apply more of my own tonic," Grant shares. He has scaled back some of his professional commitments in order to give his own marriage more attention. "My wife and I aren't part of some mythical group of untroubled people with no problems to sort through. What I've learned from watching and trying to help other people with their relationships, I am beginning to use more right here at home."

Intimacy is an elusive goal in any relationship, not something that happens automatically just because we want it to. It seems, sometimes, that the closer you get to another person, the more clearly you see the real obstacles and issues that keep you apart. Whether friend or spouse, parent or child, we call to each other "across the incalculable gulfs that separate us."[2]

FORGING NEW CONNECTIONS

The middle years of life are one place where the "incalculable gulfs" become particularly apparent. This can be a challenging time in any relationship, because unresolved issues usually become more evident as a couple nears the magic years around forty. Women in their late thirties are especially susceptible to feelings of loneliness, even in marriage—a type of relational estrangement called "feeling alone together."[3]

Another reason midlife can produce stress in a relationship is that this is when men and women each experience a drop in hormone levels, with differing responses. When a woman realizes she has had her last child, she begins to look harder outside the nest for places to channel her energy and drive. Emotionally and physically, she is ready to take on the world. Often this new confidence and motivation coincides with the opposite response in her husband. He has been making his way through the asphalt jungle for years. Just about the time his wife is gearing up to take flight, his thoughts are turning toward home, toward the admission of his own relational needs.[4]

In other words, the rhythms of their achieving and nurturing drives head in opposite directions. They may miss each other totally, each becoming an obstacle in the other's path. Hopefully, they will meet on a whole new level of understanding and support. Forging new and deeper connections is a common task for couples at this stage in life. For many, the time seems ripe for change.

From our earliest days, Stacy and I had quietly prided ourselves in how much we could accomplish as a couple. We were both hard drivers, two workhorses yoked together in a common cause. Because it was so important to move full steam ahead, we learned how to avoid any messy scenes between us, especially anything emotional. We learned how *not* to need each other too badly. The tears, the arguments, the drawn-out discussions—they do tend to slow a person down. We agreed, in the tacit, unspoken way that couples do, that we simply did not have time for that.

If ever a hint arose that something might get out of hand, I pulled the old writer's trick. "Let's stop talking here," I would say to Stacy. "It's obvious this is upsetting us both. I'll just write out the way I see this situation on a piece of paper and then you'll have the benefit of my perspective objectively." So I would write up my thoughts like a lawyer's brief, carefully deleting any potentially emotional word from the text.

The problem came when I awoke in one summer of disturbing discontent. Something was missing between us, something I couldn't even put into words. I admired Stacy's talents, but more and more he just seemed like a familiar old friend I lived with. I couldn't *feel* much of anything.

If we had come together to accomplish a common task, we had succeeded admirably. If marriage was a goal, rather than a relationship, we met the requirements. We enjoyed many of the same pursuits and our values were remarkably similar. But somewhere in all our busyness, we had let go of the emotional connections between us. It was the matters of the heart, the very essence of our relationship, that we had both neglected.

These were some of the conclusions we reached when we began to take stock after almost twenty years of marriage. We could both sense that we had begun to drift apart and it was time to take a hard look at the reasons why.

Sometimes it seems that this stage in life is especially designed by God to force that kind of reflection. The gap between the great hopes of our past and the hard realities of the present motivates the soul searching that brings about real change and personal growth. We have the potential to forge new connections through a variety of means, but three in particular play a significant role.

Confronting Our Fear of Intimacy

Sometimes I think that the challenge of intimacy can best be likened to what it's like to talk, to kiss, to connect with someone through thermopane glass. In a close relationship there is a translucent wall between you where you can see and hear and watch the other person, but only on rare occasions are you able to actually break through the barrier and really touch.

The reason that real intimacy is so difficult is that the closer we come to each other, the deeper we are taken into the territory of our own worst fears. Love, if it's real, can always be rejected, and the possibility of rejection or ridicule from a person who matters to us is not a pleasant one. Ambivalence sets in. On one level, the prospect of intimacy entices us, woos us, invites us to partake. Yet on a deeper level, fear begs us to play it safe. Instinctively we know that intimacy holds a high price because of the effort and risk involved in being that vulnerable.

In nearly every case, though, those risks are the very ones we need to take. When Stacy and I began to open our lives to each other on a deeper level, our actions were exactly counter to the safe, secure habits we spent years perfecting in order to keep our distance. All of a sudden, the rules were changing, and both of us were thrown off balance. We learned to lean less on sheer logic and to trust, instead, our instincts and intuition. It took determination to face the places where we had let each other down, and time to get honest about what was really bothering us. We had our share of messy scenes with no carefully worded lawyer's brief to stand in the way. And somewhere in the midst of it all, we forged some new connections that have reminded us again of the real reasons we married each other in the first place.

It means new life to a relationship when these kinds of little breakthroughs happen. Slowly but surely, you start to make connections in the very places where harm has been done in the past.

Linking Arms

Midlife can also mean the chance to pull together against all the odds that would normally defeat you. Aging parents, resistant teenagers, a struggling business—the stress can become the pressure that drives you closer together, that moves you beyond a simple I-do-this-you-do-that kind of relationship. This is one of the insights that Ted and his wife, Anne, have discovered as they've combined their efforts to make a go of their floral distribution business.

At first, the fact that they were partners in a business as well as a marriage seemed as much of a problem as it was a blessing. Ted always dealt with their floral clients, and managed a sale and supply team of twelve employees. Anne, who was an artistic person by nature, helped him create a display room with more style and flair than any other supplier in town. But she also knew the state of his accounts receivable.

When the business first started to take a downward turn, they spent hours together discussing how they should respond—planning new initiatives, figuring out what they could do without, second-guessing their decision to start this business in the first place.

As the weeks turned into months, though, and the downward turn became a sinking spiral, the talk got less and less. "We just seemed to leave each other with more worry than when we started, and neither of us needed that," remembers Ted.

But the loneliness that was taking hold in their relationship was heavier than the stack of bills on Ted's desk. The weight was too much to carry alone. Finally one of them sat down with the other and said, "This is ridiculous. We've got to stay in this together—sink or swim."

What they feel now is that the adversity of the last five years has made them a real team, in the best sense. Making a go of this business has been the right melding of their talents and gifts. It has taken everything they've had to give. They have each come to respect and appreciate the other on a new level.

"I always knew that Ted was a natural leader," Anne says, "but that ability got overlooked during the time when we were just hanging on month-to-month." She has had the benefit of standing back and watching his leadership abilities be refined under pressure. "I see Ted as the leader with a towel around his waist. He's not the slightest bit enamored with title and position. His natural strength has come back better than ever."

Ted credits Anne's innovation and ingenuity in design as the deciding human factor in keeping them over the edge of solvency. "People come in and take pictures of our design floor now. We're not just another floral business with boxes of fresh cut and dried flowers to pick from," he says. Her flair and style have shaped their niche in the marketplace.

Both of them have had the chance to watch each other up close through some difficult situations. They know where they've failed. They also know they've seen the other "do some pretty amazing things through some pretty tough times."

They are beginning to see some of the benefits that are theirs as a result of facing this kind of adversity together. "For one thing, we've gained a much broader understanding of the whole idea of roles in marriage," Ted explains. "Our lives are so integrated that the lines between who's-the-leader and who's-the-follower have kind of dissolved. We've just linked arms."

When they look back to where they were spiritually and relationally ten years ago, they see how far they've come. "Sometimes I think that if we've made it through this together, we can make it through almost anything. It's a good feeling," Anne says.

The intimacy they're experiencing now is what comes when a couple weathers the stress and strain by choosing to pull together, and by capitalizing on the individual strengths that each person contributes to the whole.

Giving Each Other the Space to Grow

Another route by which two people deepen intimacy contains a note of irony. Instead of enlarging the points on which their relationship overlaps, they begin to encourage each other's development toward their own individual bent.

The task that young married couples face is that of bonding together. After years of choosing their own preferences and schedule and idiosyncrasies, they learn to bend with the wishes of another. If all goes as it should, two individuals move from independence to interdependence.

As a couple matures, however, another set of forces is at work. The emphasis switches slightly. You begin, once again, to discover yourself and your mate as individuals. Now you experience not just the unity in your diversity, but also the diversity in your unity.[5] You begin to see your mate as an *individual* who is not like you, and not traveling exactly the same path as you.

When your own individuality is no longer so easily endangered, you are better able to give your mate the space to grow. You stop trying so hard to script the other person into what you need them to be. It's like saying, on an emotional level, "I don't have to make you be like me in order for me to feel good about myself." The irony is that you grow closer as you set each other free as individuals.

This is the process Grant and his wife find themselves in at this point in their lives. For years, their relationship has revolved around his growing client load and the needs of their four children. Frequent moves that have produced more acquaintances than friends have added to a sense of isolation. His wife often feels that her focus has become so narrowed over the years, that she has little to contribute to their relationship. She feels lost in the shuffle. So Grant has begun to encourage her to discover her own interests and talents. He finds that she needs confidence boosters and that his opinion and support really matter to her. "I'm starting to see how much more multi-faceted this woman is than what I realized," he says, "and it's adding a new dimension to our relationship."

So while many couples deepen their relationship by encouraging each other's individuality, or by facing outward adversity together and confronting their own inner fears, still, "a perfect relationship" is never ours this side of heaven. We are forever in process, moving toward a desire that will remain, in the deepest sense, unfulfilled. Even the best we now experience leaves us still longing for more.

Perhaps, what we learn after all these years is how much the world of relationships defies prescriptions and how-to formulas. In the final analysis, intimacy is more something we stumble upon than a state of being we can orchestrate—a peculiar kind of grace that comes long after we've searched the motivations of our own hearts and made some changes.

PRIVATE TUTORING IN RELATIONSHIPS

In some ways, marriage is a microcosmic view of potential intimacy, a miniature laboratory for other close relationships. Martin Luther called marriage a school in which our character is built, a place where what we learn about releasing our grip on our oversized expectations and embracing another person for the individual he or she is, spills over into other relationships.

Inside that laboratory, the very impasses which often serve to undermine intimacy in a relationship contain as much potential to make it something new and rich and desirable. In his book, *The Road Less Traveled,* M. Scott Peck writes about what a basically hopeful sign it is when a couple falls out of love. This is when they have the chance "to initiate the work of real loving . . . it is when a couple falls out of love they may begin to really love."[6] We need to be the most determined at just the time when we are most tempted to give up. Or as the women's columnist Judith Viorst quips, "One advantage of marriage is that when you fall out of love with him or he falls out of love with you, it keeps you together until you fall in love again."[7]

Just as individuals go through passages, so marriages do as well. We weather life together. Sometimes we forget that the same relationship that began with vows and wedding cake edges forward, day by day, to a hill where a little green tent is pitched by a graveside. There is not long in between.

Stacy and I rarely make big occasions out of the anniversaries between those two events, but two years ago we took an exception. We decided to cash in airline mileage on a special trip to England to celebrate our fifteen years together.

The grandparents came to take care of their grandchildren, and we gathered our travel brochures and camera and headed off for a week. Little Cotswald cottages, tea and scones at 4 o'clock—this was supposed to be the trip to beat all trips. And we did have a good time. Eight whole days without a children's carpool or soccer practice can do a lot for any couple. But about the middle of the week, I had to admit that our trip hardly resembled the pictures in the advertisements.

For one thing, the prices were almost double those we remembered from ten years previous. Rain or unexpected crowds cancelled a number of our plans. And those little Cotswald cottages had some beds that were made for two of the seven dwarfs. We spent a few nights head to toe, and one, at least, with Stacy snoring peacefully on the floor beside me. Not exactly a second honeymoon.

Not until we were headed home did it strike me how fitting this trip to England had been to celebrate a marriage. Fifteen years before we set out on a lifetime journey together, every bit as starry-eyed as we had been just a week before. Instead of travel brochures, we had books and tapes and big ideas on the subject. We knew, or thought we knew, how to settle conflict, and what intimacy was supposed to look like. In other words, we had a lot of knowledge, but not much understanding.

We had not counted on spending half our marriage in school. Or selling a home for less than we bought it for. Or the changes in each other that required new, sometimes painful, adjustments. There is just so much that no one understands until they've been there.

Our trip—and our marriage—had been different than we expected. And in both cases, we had a tendency to let individual events and ruffled feathers obscure the overall picture. Having children and renovating houses, straining to find the right career niches—our relationship was more than the sum of those parts, just as our vacation to England couldn't be defined by the places we visited. In both cases, there was something far more significant happening than the events themselves.

The point was, we had made the trip together. We were beginning to learn something about what it meant to keep company on the colder nights.

Like many people in our generation, Stacy and I had hoped to find ecstasy in each other's arms. When we found something less than that, we did not know what to do with the disappointment for a long time. It took a while to see that we had actually stumbled on to something better than bliss—a love that is valuable precisely because it has been costly.

Not long after we returned from England, we were in McDonald's, which is still our children's favorite place to go. Our kids were busy dividing the french fries piece by greasy piece lest one outdo the other, and Stacy was putting away his traditional Big Mac. I was drawn instead to a retired couple seated right across the aisle. These days, old couples who look like they have weathered the years together well hold a peculiar fascination for me.

I think this couple had chosen this spot in the road to take a break. Two cups of coffee were all their table held.

With a burr haircut that stuck up like a mass of silver pins, the old farmer was thick in the middle of some tale. His wife stirred cream and sugar into both their cups, a habit so well ingrained it was second nature. She listened, not saying all that much, a smile playing about a face that was lined with age.

They had the kind of easy familiarity with each other where one sentence means a paragraph and the silences aren't heavy. I was struck by how thoroughly at home they seemed in each other's company. And I could not help but notice the way he reached for her hand on the way back out to their pickup truck.

I turned back to Stacy, who was now in the final stages of arbitration over exactly who had gotten most of the fries. This was the man I wanted to grow old with—this fair-haired German with the mustache and the iron stomach. Thirty years from now, I'd like to stroll across a parking lot and have this guy reach for my hand.

Neither of us has lived up to all of the other's hopes. When it comes to whether or not I have fulfilled Stacy's fantasies, he has, no doubt, been forced to use some imagination. Then again, every time I've tried to make him my knight in shining armor, we've both fallen off our horse. We've wasted enough time on smaller matters.

Our marriage is in a passage somewhere between the Beach Boys and Lawrence Welk—a little old for good vibrations and not quite ready for bubble music. We're somewhere in between. Who knows how much time there is left?

I only know that I want to dance while the music is still being played.

CHAPTER 10

Making It
When Less Starts to Seem Like Enough

When I was a kid, I thought this was all just the beginning of the good times. I thought things would just get better from that point on.

Marie Callum, 35

———————————◆———————————

Tucked away in some little corner of our minds there harbors a picture of the good life. We collect images and store them there, like the little girl who flips through a dozen magazines until she gathers just the assortment of advertisements that strike her fancy. A dream home, a romantic vacation, a job that requires a sharp-looking suit, the right schools for the kids, whatever. We all know the basic building blocks for the standard American dream.

Most of us would hate to admit that there is any correlation between that dream and our faith and expectations of God. The "abundant life" found in Jesus did not necessarily mean an abundance of stuff. It was not the same as the good life. We knew that.

The problem is that the idealistic period of time that inflated our expectations of life coincided with the onset of the prosperity gospel. This was the idea that affluence and success were the marks of God's special blessing on his obedient children—a premise easily challenged by Scripture. The lives of Jeremiah and Paul and Jesus Christ hardly fit anyone's profile for prosperity. Unfortunately, though, the prosperity gospel fit well with many current, but temporary financial trends of the time—the oil boom in the '70s and the inflated stock market of the '80s. While most of us could spot the error, it nevertheless played havoc in our subconscious. Maybe God's blessing could indeed be measured in dollars and cents. Perhaps God did want me rich. Maybe I really am what I own.

The last twenty-five years have contained numerous financial cycles, periods of expansion and prosperity followed closely by recession and cutbacks. As a result, many of us have felt whiplashed by the rollercoaster nature of those cycles, confused as to exactly what it *does* mean to experience the goodness of God in our lives.

Whether we connected our material dreams with our faith or not, the good life is getting harder and harder to get. While our Depression-era parents considered a college education or owning your own car to be something of a privilege—the "icing" on their cake—for us, those things were just part of the cake. The good life was that plus a whole lot more. "Did we really set out to have it all?" I asked a friend once. "Not exactly," she replied. "I just want a little bit of all of it."

We are the generation that spawned Donald Trump. He is one of us. And like Donald, many of us have experienced the contraction of our dreams, rather than the continued expansion we hoped for. The statistics on our generation, taken as a whole, are somewhat sobering. While five to ten percent of us actually lived the lives depicted on slick magazine covers, the vast majority of us are not projected to fare nearly as well as our parents have. We have not automatically gotten richer as we have grown older, the way wine improves with age. The average income of a person aged twenty-five to thirty-four has been declining for ten years straight. There are forty thousand Ph.D.s in our generation who cannot get a job in their field. Fewer jobs, fewer promotions, lower relative wages—the litany goes on and on. Maybe the Rolling Stones were right—you can't always get what you want.

Many of us stand straddled between more options and fewer means. "I've got the education and the ability to do a variety of jobs," explains a man in his early thirties, who has spent the last several years trying to find his niche in sales. "I'm not like my father. I don't have to spend my life in one job working in a bank like he did."

Instead, there are a host of different arenas in which he could maximize his talents. But he hadn't counted on how quickly those options could dry up in a down-turned economy. "Trying to match up available jobs with my skills and my mortgage payment hasn't been easy," he says. He can see what it is he wants. It's within his reach, but always a little beyond his grasp.

Scenarios like this one, repeated dozens of times, explain why fully a third of our generation is disappointed in what they have achieved thus far in life.[1] There is a persistent feeling that "I ought to be farther along than I am." How much farther? Research shows that most of us live by the "25 percent rule."[2] We need 25 percent more money or status or achievement to feel successful. And success, for a generation for whom the "icing" has become the "cake," is a constantly moving thing.

We get caught between the life we had and the life we would like to provide for our children. One woman, whose father and husband are both small town dentists, mirrored well this kind of squeeze. "Our children look at their grandfather in his sportscar coming home from some big trip and they want to know why we're still driving a station wagon," she says. She tries to explain that their father is as good a dentist as their grandfather, but that times are just different.

"When I was growing up," she remembers, "my parents set aside $700 a year and we toured a different *region* of the country every summer. Now we could hardly take our kids to an average motel at the beach for a week on that amount."

For the most part she was not too bothered by the

discrepancy in her husband's income and her father's—until she reached her late thirties. "Before then, I just assumed it was all up ahead, around the next corner," she says. "Lately, I've started to realize that we may never get to the place, like my parents, where we can just coast."

But no matter what we have or have not achieved thus far in life, many of us arrive in our thirties with a curious sense of deflation. After graduate school, after we've had a few children, after we've redecorated the house, then what? What's next? we ask. Surely there is more.

"I was content to move from place to place while my husband finished medical school and his residency," confides a wife who has packed and unpacked too many boxes in her day. After years of the gypsy life, they settled down in a small town in Virginia's Shenandoah Valley. Her husband put his diplomas on the wall and a brass name plate on the door. They bought a new home in a nice neighborhood and put the children in school. "Then," she says, "it was like we turned to each other and said, This is it?" This was it.

Sooner or later we lose faith in the idea that one more achievement, one more degree will finally put us "over the top," and we will never again feel like the junior high kid with gum stuck in his braces. "I was finally able to open my own law firm in the town I grew up in," says a man who paid his dues working for someone else for ten years. The thrill didn't last long, though. "When all is said and done," he explains, "I really own a shop on main street where I sell law advice. It's not all that special. I'm not too different from a kid with his lemonade stand."

No matter how much or how little we have partaken of the dream, there is still an insistent urge to experience the parts that are missing. If we have excelled in accomplishments, then we may be searching for relationships. And if friends and family abound, then we are looking for ways to test our possibilities to achieve. Sometimes, what we don't have looks far more attractive than what we do have.

Cheryl Merser, in her book about growing up and growing older in this generation, talks about how she realized that she had a job in a New York City publishing house that others envied. The book she had just written adorned her coffee table. But the farther she got into her thirties, the more lonely she was becoming. "So what if I had written a book?" she says. "Now I looked at my book, sitting on my coffee table, in disgust. You can't kiss a book good morning, or make love to it at night, tuck it in and read it a story, or carry its picture around in your wallet. You can't even wash clothes in it. What good is a book?"[3]

So it is that many of us arrive in our late thirties and early forties with our images of the good life either evaporating or taking on an entirely new shape. We scale down our expectations, or redefine them, and try to disconnect our ideas about the American Dream from the promises of God.

MORE PRESSURE, HARDER CHOICES

So what do you do when you wake up one day and realize the big chunk of your life is behind you and you still haven't *arrived?* Not in that carved-in-stone way you thought you would, anyway. Your life doesn't measure up to the mural you had painted in that tiny corner of your mind.

That's not an easy idea to face when you can also hear the relentless ticking of your own internal clock. After all, whatever it is that you're going to do or be or achieve or experience, you had better get after it. Time is running out. It's too late to be a trapeze artist or a belly dancer or a nun. Some possibilities are already past tense. One life is all you get, one trip around the gameboard, and you aren't allowed to go past "Go" again and collect another $200.

All of this adds up to pressure. More pressure to achieve and acquire, to hang on to a job you dislike for the security it represents, to buy when you should rent, to build when you'd be wiser to remodel. The modern workplace and lifestyle exact a high emotional toll, as psychologist Douglas LaBier found when he studied the lives of 230 people between the ages of twenty-five and forty-seven.[4] Our age group is overrun with anxiety, burnout, and the stress that comes from straining to reach the elusive target of "making it," one that moves as soon as we get anywhere close.

"I wish I could remember how to relax," says a man nearing forty who wonders if he'll ever get out of the middle management pool. He admits that he frequently flips to the radio station that plays "Venus in Blue Jeans" and other classic pieces of serious musicians. "It takes me back to an era in my life when I could spend days with my feet in the sand, a beer in my hand, listening to the waves pound the beach like there was no tomorrow," he says. Now he can hardly find his way to a beach and when he does, he's got a briefcase of work under one arm and his children's rafts under the other. By the time he unwinds it's time to head for home.

This is the point, in the middle of life, that we cross an invisible line and our focus shifts from how many years we have lived to how many years we may have left. Life takes on that "last chance" feeling. If you ever hope to get the degree you wish you already had, or raise the venture capital for your own business, or uproot to a totally new location, there seems no better time than now. Things that were just possibilities before, now appear urgent as you weigh the *risks versus the benefits perceived.* The question becomes, how much present security are you willing to give up in order to reach out for something different?

"Suppose I never do leave teaching—which seems like a rut I've worn too smooth—and go back to school in computer programming? Can I make it another twenty-five years in this field, and if I do, will I be a dehydrated fruit when I do? Can our budget stretch far enough to let me try something new?" A hundred questions like these clamor for answers because the answers affect not just our own life, but the lives of everyone close to us.

As our responsibilities in life increase and our physical stamina wanes, we face some hard choices. Opportunities we have worked years for may unfold at the same time other demands on our life and challenges with our children reach a high water mark. We shift into overdrive and rev up the old adrenalin once again.

But your body refuses to cooperate. If you burn the candle at both ends for too long at this point in life, you may find there's no wick left to catch fire. It's like your body intercepts your brain. "No matter how hard I try," complains one nurse with three children, "I can't push any harder than I'm already pushing. There's nothing left to push with."

Somewhere between the ages of thirty-five and forty-five, our responsibilities collide headlong with our capacity to perform. We are hamstrung between *the demands on our life versus our capacity to meet those demands.* The responsibilities have increased but our stamina probably has not. When that happens, the real tests of character and values come to fore. "What will I have to jettison?" we ask. "What do I want to keep and what do I need to let go of?"

Most of us don't see these choices coming before they are upon us, nor do we anticipate the pressure that goes along with them. That's what Grant realized when he established his psychiatric practice outside a large metropolitan city. He had expected to bury himself in the task of sorting out the problems of hurting people who came for help. But fifteen years ago, when he chose psychiatry as his specialty, he had not foreseen the day when someone who could integrate Christianity and psychology would be in such demand.

Now, his weekly mail includes invitations to speak and to give seminars on a variety of topics that genuinely interest him. He is nearing a place in his own development where he feels he has something to say. He has always wanted to publish and that no longer looks like a pipe dream.

His only problem is that his opportunities are coinciding with a time when his four children are quickly growing up. They have their own dreams, dreams that need a father's encouragement. Sometimes he feels pulled apart at the seams. "I can't afford to get where I want to go at my kids' expense," he says. "I see too much of that in my office every day." He knows that if you have to steal from your kids in order to make it, in the long run, you may lose on both counts.

Still, he often feels caught in a vise, afraid that if he passes up these opportunities, he may not have others to choose from later when he has more time. He admits that he is the one who usually pays the price, through lack of sleep and days off, for trying to keep too much going at once. He realizes that he is living without a margin and that his days of being able to do so are numbered.

Grant is facing up to the fact that while the demands on him have increased, he has a limited reservoir of energy to meet them. Like him, many of us experience more pressure in this stage in life to establish some clear goals that help us let go or postpone lesser priorities. The good life is a lesser life if it forces us to run twice as fast just to keep up.

HOW TO KNOW WHEN YOU'VE MADE IT

If someone had ever asked me what was the predominant image on that mural of the good life in my mind, I would have had to say, simply, a house. Not just any house, though—a turn-of-the century house with a few antiques and wood floors and a staircase. I wasn't thinking *big* necessarily; a cozy place with gables and high ceilings would do fine. Over the years, with each of our moves, this picture has become clearer in my mind.

Only with every move, we seemed to acquire new skill in our ability to choose a housing market higher than the one we were leaving. Like so many Americans and so many people our age, our tastes always exceeded our means. Just by a little, but then there are times when a little seems like a lot.

Moving back east to North Carolina was the hardest move of all. Never had I seen such a wealth of old houses to choose from. Why, if I kept redefining my concept of old, we could buy a house that pre-dated World War I, or the Civil War, or for that matter, the original revolt from England. Just how old a house did I want, anyway?

Everyday I went out looking at houses, I felt like I was on a great treasure hunt. I lay awake at night plotting my strategy to transform the wonderful old monstrosity I had seen that day into a restored masterpiece fit for the covers of *Southern Living*.

Like a child in a candy store, though, I kept forgetting to count the change in my purse. My husband and the loan officer at the bank had to jog my memory. We could not afford a turn-of-the-century home. Again. It was that simple. After five moves and two other tries, we were going to have to buy a house in *this* century, and probably the most recent half at that. By the time we could afford the kind of house with gables and a staircase, I might well be wallpapering the foyer from my electric wheelchair.

An old house, restored to the luster of a warmer era, had always represented for me a place of safety and security. That was "making it" in my mind—the invitation to kick off my shoes, sit back, and rest a spell.

Everyone, I'm convinced, has some picture, some dream that lures them forward and promises relief from the daily grind. Those who are skilled in advertising and marketing know how to best tap into those images, and then add a little paint on our brush. They help us turn a desire into a full-fledged need.

It is possible, however, in this world of pressure and hard choices and doused hopes, for us to paint over some of the good–life mural in our minds. There are unexpected places where less starts to seem like more.

When We Find a Different Measuring Stick

Often hidden in the rubble of a disappointed dream, there lies a treasure or two that we could never have seen while we were so bent on realizing our hope. One of those concerns the inner criteria by which we measure success. Our ideals change as our hopes take on a different shape.

When Ted was at the height of his financial crisis, for instance, and was convinced that his business might go under, he kept hoping that God would come to his rescue on a grand scale. But the "miracle" never came. Instead, he hung on for months, with finances the ever-present issue and failure looming large before him.

Only as time gave him perspective could he begin to see that the business was making forward progress, inch by inch. Answers to his prayer in this regard were coming in dribbles, not downpours; in such small increments, in fact, that Ted could not rest on the laurels of being the "young, successful entrepreneur" he had once hoped to become.

When, finally, he was allowed some breathing room and finances were not a constant matter of survival, he found a curious thing had taken place. He had developed a new criteria for what success looked and felt like. He was holding a different yardstick.

"I noticed, for the first time, that I had grown to feel

immense pleasure in the work we were doing. In a world where Madonna gets rave reviews, we were offering a product of real quality, and I began to let myself enjoy that," he says. "I've come to think that there is a peculiar pleasure God gives a person when he's in his element, his niche—*a kind of joy in the work itself.*"

He is also beginning to reap the benefits among his employees from all the months of having to pull together. In the process of learning how to resolve conflict, they have become a team. The pleasure in those relationships is, again, something Ted had never before counted in his concept of success. Should the business climate improve, Ted feels like he has the foundation necessary to take advantage of it. He admits that had he been able to reach his earlier business goals and spin off new floral franchises, he would probably never have slowed down long enough to savor any of this.

In *Downshifting,* business writer Amy Saltzman chronicles the lives of people in our generation who have made conscious choices to redefine the way they measure success. The plateauer, the back-tracker, the career shifter, the self-employer, and the urban escapee represent five kinds of people who decided to leave the fast lane in favor of a saner, more satisfying lifestyle. Saltzman uses their examples to challenge us to "reinvent" our notions of success and to adopt new "success imagery" that allows us to slow down and enjoy more of life.

There is a good life that Ted's experiencing—it's just not the one he had expected. His story is an example of what often happens when reality does not measure up to our expectations. As we let go of some of the false images in our minds, we find we develop a new, truer definition of success.

When We Discover What We Really Want

There is another place where less can begin to seem like more, and that is on the level of our deepest desires.

Sometimes our dreams, especially the ones built on advertising pictures of the good life, serve only to camouflage our true desires. I may think, for instance, that I want a Victorian gingerbread house with lace doilies and the smell of cinnamon throughout. That's what I have been conditioned to think I want, anyway. But in reality, if I probe a little deeper, I am really after the warmth and intimacy of the relationships that I perceive exist in such a picture. If I ask myself what I *really* want, I am led to the intangibles that can't be acquired like items on a shopping list.

The problem is that most of us are so driven in our pursuit of that enticing dream in the back of our minds, we don't stop long enough to identify what we really want. Our energy is consumed in the effort to realize our dreams, to finally come to the elusive point where we feel like we've arrived. Our subconscious question is, How can I get there—wherever *there* is? And we ask it so persistently that we never get to the questions that follow. We don't get the chance to move from "How can I get there?" to "Where am I trying to get?" and finally, "What if I did?"

So we fall prey to all sorts of advertising come-ons. I think of one, for example, a personal invitation in the mail that many people our age receive. This one is not engraved but it tries hard to be impressive and if by chance we don't answer it the first time, we will receive another opportunity soon. American Express would like to place a plastic card in our hand that can open the doors to all the things we think we ever wanted.

They know the right words to say. They are sending you this special invitation because "you are a person who will appreciate this most honored and prestigious financial instrument . . . the sense of self-esteem, the recognition, and the security that come from carrying the world's most respected card." Security, prestige, recognition. Here, supposedly, is your ticket.

I happened to read these words over my husband's shoulder on the day they landed in our mailbox and together we both smiled. "It's nice to be pursued, if only for our money," he mused.

The question occurred to me, "What would you want if you had the cars and the trips and the long business lunches this card seems to promise?" What I actually said was, "What would you want then?" I watched him chew on that for a while, waiting for his response and not even sure what my own would be.

His answer caught me off guard. I expected to hear him say something outlandish, like a kid with three wishes and a genie in his bottle. After he had gotten the dreams that little card symbolized, he said that he'd probably pack up and take the kids camping.

"Camping?" I said. "You would take the kids camping?"

Yes, he assured me. But that wasn't all. "I guess I'd be looking for some good friends, for a sense of impact on my world, maybe a deeper connection with the Lord." And for good measure, an expanded schedule of racquetball—something as uncomplicated as a good chance to sweat.

This was what he would really want?

When he finished, we both stopped. Like two minds in syncopated rhythm, it hit us. What we really wanted— genuine relationships, a sense of impact, time to enjoy life—did not require a plastic card to acquire. Maybe we had gotten so attached to our dreams along the way that we forgot the point to them. Perhaps we were only beginning to uncover our true desires. In other words, what we really wanted was more accessible than we thought. In fact, *it was an awful lot of what we had.*

Our generation and those coming after us are often called "the disenfranchised generation." The good life we were raised to think we would inherit is slipping through our fingers like sand. The problem is not that we want too much. Our desires are not too strong; they are more often uninformed. It seems to take almost half a lifetime and the disappointment of some of our dreams to come to terms with what we really want out of life.

Perhaps our generation, whether by choice or default, will be the first to redesign our ideas about what exactly constitutes the good life. Maybe we will be the ones to admit that even a beach in Tahiti is pretty barren without the peace of mind and depth of relationships to fill out the scene. And that if you had to choose, at least you would know what choice to make, because you know what it is you *really* want.

Sometimes these days I find myself sitting on our front porch out under the shade of tall pine trees. The red brick of our ranch home frames a Carolina blue sky and seems to beg for geraniums and impatiens plants to line its borders.

I stare at gutters, not gables and the only staircase is the one that leads right in the front door. Inside there are offices in strange places, a kitchen being remodeled, and three bedrooms in need of fresh paint. A few antiques and wood floors are spaced throughout, but basically, this house represents another compromise. It is not my dream home; its bricks were laid too recently. It dates back to the wrong war—the one in Vietnam.

My own ideas about the good life are changing, slowly. While this house fails to live up to the one on the mural in my mind, and it's not my picture of the good life— still, who knows? If we stay here another ten years we will finally own a turn-of-the-century home.

The turn of the next century.

CHAPTER 11

An Honest Faith
Moving Beyond the Simple Answers

You've got to experience the bottom of life falling out a couple of times and God somehow being there in the midst of it. All of that happens in your thirties and that's where a person really encounters God.

Roger Randall, 41

———————◆———————

Disappointments come in all kinds of different shapes and sizes, weights and measures. Some merely glance off you sideways, like tiny beads of sleet on the arm of a stadium jacket. You can feel the ping, but it's not bad enough to run for cover. But other disappointments penetrate. They cut to the core like a knife, leaving you with the feeling that you have been split apart and left in sections.

Letting go of old dreams is, for anyone, an inevitable part of maturing. No one gets through life with all their dreams intact. But when a particular hope was fueled and carried forward on faith—when it's hard to tell where the dream stops and your faith starts—that kind of disappointment is no ordinary loss. It is the deepest disappointment of all, and it strikes a double blow because it threatens our understanding of God.

Susan's story is a good example of the kind of broken dream that challenges the foundations of a person's faith and ability to trust God. When she met and married Jim, she felt she was pursuing a direction that had all the marks of God's blessing. Their relationship was built on common beliefs and shared values, undergirded by the sense that God had something special in mind for the two of them as a couple. They had a solid spiritual foundation from which to build a lifetime together.

Yet within the first few years of marriage, Susan became more and more aware that there was also something chipping away at that foundation. Jim's struggles with his father, his inner restlessness and frustration only seemed to grow, as though it were fed from a spring whose source neither of them could locate.

During their last six months together, Jim's personality began to change drastically. He started devising elaborate means to be everywhere but home. He had another life—business, nightclubs, and who-knows-what else— and it became obvious that Susan was not invited to be a part. More and more, they were living in two separate worlds and the wall between them was not one Susan could scale alone.

When Susan was six months pregnant with their second child, Jim told her that he would stay long enough for the baby to be born. But then, he wanted a place of his own. He was planning to move out.

Kelsey, their second little girl, arrived on schedule, an easy baby with bright eyes and full of life. There were moments in the hospital when Susan was sure she saw a hint of tenderness in Jim's face when he held her. She continued to pray, more hopefully now, that God would intervene in their lives through this tiny infant.

Jim brought everyone home, posed for a few pictures, and played the part of a dutiful daddy—for a few weeks anyway. But his old restlessness, that subterranean anger, returned and this time, the normal family forces that would keep him home only seemed to repel him all the more for their intensity. He was living on the edge.

Jim left quietly one day when Susan had taken both girls to the doctor. She found the note on the kitchen table and his closet emptied of its contents. Her first response was that for once, Jim had been totally true to his word. He had stayed long enough for Kelsey to be born.

A protective numbness set in, one that prevented Susan from feeling the full effect of what was happening to her. For a while, she let herself get lost in the constant demands of a toddler and a nursing baby. But her money was running out and it was clear that Jim was filing for divorce. When her parents offered to drive down from Oregon and help her pack to move back there, she reluctantly agreed. She didn't know what else to do.

The full weight of reality fell on her as she was turning into the driveway of the home she had grown up in. She had trouble finding the car door handle for the tears that were streaming down her face. This was not the way you were supposed to come home—with two small children in the back seat and your father pulling a U-Haul with the contents of your home behind you. It was like waking up to a bad dream.

Susan slowly began to establish a new life there. She got a job in public relations for a pharmaceutical firm and her mother helped out with the girls. In haphazard form, Susan managed to put back a few of the pieces of her life. But underneath the edges of that cut-and-paste job, she was raw on the inside. She felt alone and abandoned by her husband—and on a more profound level, by God. Why had he seemed present in their courtship and so absent during the last two years of their marriage? How had he let this happen?

Those were the kind of questions brewing inside Susan but she tried to ignore them. She stayed clear of the Christian community, afraid that her disillusionment would show. Besides, the sound of church music had a disturbing tendency to make her cry. She found herself unable to turn to God. Just a look in his direction stirred memories of her relationship with Jim—warm memories of old times when they prayed together, of how right their relationship had felt, of all the spiritual hopes they had shared. Somehow her faith, her ability to trust God, was tied up in those dreams and she had no idea how to unravel such a tangled knot.

She tried not to think too hard, but sometimes, her dreams betrayed her, as though her mind continued to search for resolution while she slept. One dream, in particular, stayed with her during all the months that her divorce dragged on. In her dream, she saw a woman dressed in a white robe go past her bedroom door. Her face was radiant, like the spirit of God, and there were many people following her. Then in a few minutes, Susan saw the same woman come by her door again. This time she hobbled by with the help of a cane, her face drawn and distorted with incredible bitterness and hate.

At that point, Susan bolted awake from her dream and almost by reflex found herself praying. "Oh, God," she said, "don't let me become that bitter old woman."

Susan's dream of a warm, intimate marriage ended, as many do, in divorce. And when any marriage ends, there is heartache and grief. But because the steps that led her toward her dream were steps of *faith,* filled with the patchwork of answered prayer and special circumstances, Susan was left with troubling doubts and questions. A marriage made in heaven is just not supposed to end up in a divorce court.

For those of us who know what it is to wed hope to faith, we empathize with the inner struggle that resonates beneath the pain of such a loss. The idea of trusting God was the anchor to which many in our generation tied their dreams. In this kind of disappointment, we are left with one question—if we let go of our dream, or if it is wrested from us, then will we lose, along with it, our ability to trust God in any true measure? As one woman voiced after years of infertility and miscarriages, ending in a hysterectomy: "I would not have dared to hope so hard or so long except that I thought God was in it.

When I realized that he wasn't, I felt as though I had been dancing with a lion." She struggled not only with the loss of a dream, but with how that loss had undermined her faith as well.

When a hope is dashed that was once closely tied to the question of faith—a dilemma experienced fairly commonly in our generation—a person is left with unsettling emotions and inner turmoil. Sometimes people talk of how they feel they've lost their spiritual bearings, as though they had been led down a particular road that suddenly became a blind alley. Fog settles in, and so much of what once seemed clear and simple no longer is. This is the natural point where one would perhaps turn to God—but then again, his whereabouts have never seemed less certain. It appears as though he has defeated his own purposes and become, if not the author of our disappointment, then at least an accomplice. It all gets very confusing.

WHEN THE BOX CRUMBLES

While an experience of this nature can be trying, it nevertheless represents a critical juncture in the development of a person's faith. We are being presented with the opportunity to let go of a faith that is often, in reality, not faith at all. It is more akin to a *manageable belief system,* where faithfulness or obedience on our part seems to obligate God to bring about the desires we had in mind. Faith, as a manageable belief system, is a faith which insists. What we are asked to embrace at this juncture in life is *an open-ended trust,* where we let go of our efforts to control the outcome of following God.

Perhaps, in some ways, I am describing a kind of reconversion—a new turning, a deep inner response to a Person so "wholly other," he can't be exhausted by our concepts, our words, our imaginations, or our expectations. A Person who encourages and challenges, supports and frustrates, serves and demands. Someone different than what we had in mind, but the one we needed all along.

In many ways, this is an inevitable and much-needed turn in our spiritual journey because we all begin with constricted, one-dimensional ideas about what God is really like. I sometimes think of a wise old seminary professor I once knew who begins his class each fall, a class usually filled with bright, idealistic young men and women, by asking one simple question.

He walks into class on the first day, takes a seat on the corner of his desk with his legs swinging back and forth, and says, "Students, I have one question for you. What is God like?"

His students get their pens and notebooks in position, ready to hear the answer from the professor. But he doesn't say a word. He sits waiting for their response. In desperation, one student after another tries to fill the awkward pauses. God is love, God is justice, God is this, and God is that. The professor just sits there looking out the window, totally unimpressed. Finally, after the class has exhausted everything they ever knew or heard or conceived about God, the professor begins to speak:

"Men and women, let me tell you something," he says. "God is not like *anything.* And the tragedy is that you are going to build your little theological boxes around what you think God is like, and someday when you really need him, you're going to race to your box and open the lid and *he won't be in there."*

By this point, his class is speechless, shaking their heads in disbelief and wondering what he means. It usually takes another twenty years of maturity and the experience of having the bottom fall out a time or two before they begin to understand the wisdom in his words.

Perhaps most of us start out just like these young seminary students, wanting something predictable and sure and concretely defined. Human nature begs to construct a picture of what we think God is like, a kind of spiritual box we can fit him inside. We want a fix on God. The how-to formulas are actually comforting—tangible evidence that things will work out the way we want them to.

The kind of disappointment or letdown that jars our faith, though, also causes the walls of that box to dissolve. The spiritual territory here is uncharted, and sometimes frightening. Perhaps you took a wrong turn to have come to such a place. You don't know what else lurks in the darkness. As one friend said, "Suddenly, I realized that if the thing I feared had happened, then almost anything else was possible, too. I no longer felt safe."

"Can't I just return to the days when faith seemed sure and more simple? Can't I go back to where I was?" These are natural questions to ask. We long for a Bible study or spiritual retreat or earnest effort or *something* that would promise that old certainty. We long for faith to lose its tentative feel—to cease to feel like faith.

There is no going back, though. Our manageable belief system no longer works so well. The walls of the box— our own creation of who we think God is—begin to crumble. During this process, he often seems strangely absent, as though he has left us on our own to sort things out. Yet, in reality, what we are experiencing is the pain and confusion of letting go, not of God, but of the safe, secure confines we built to house our concept of him, our faith system. God is not a concept to be mastered, a set of prescriptions we can control. He shows himself to be much different than we thought—more loving, more exacting, more faithful.

We are being readied to take our first steps toward the freedom of relaxing in the embrace of one who is both big enough and strong enough to contain our doubts, to comfort our disappointments, and to confront our prodigal hearts.

However, in the midst of this kind of faith transition,

more than our concept of God is challenged. We may also begin to gain deeper insight into our own motivations. Disappointed hopes often reveal the stuff we're made of—both good and bad. We see how thin our own loyalties can be, how riddled with self-seeking our faith was all along.

When Ted was at his lowest point financially, only a few steps from having to declare bankruptcy, he had an encounter with a good friend that jarred him in a personal and spiritual sense. He was busy adding up figures and reviewing delinquent accounts one day, when he looked up from his desk long enough to see a new Mercedes being parked right outside his window. Out stepped his friend, Dave, with a grin on his face like a Cheshire cat.

He burst through the door of Ted's office, barely able to contain himself. "You won't believe this," he said. It seems Dave had just put together a deal for a strip shopping mall that no one thought had a ghost of a chance. He was beaming with good fortune. The commission from this should carry him through the next several years quite well.

Ted did his best to get excited with him but inside, he felt like a big fake. The whole conversation couldn't end fast enough for him. It took about a half an hour for Dave to wind down, and when Ted finally closed the door behind him, he let out a great sigh of relief. Then he quietly went back to his desk and kicked the metal trashcan against the wall as hard as he could. Why did everyone seem to have the magic formula but him? Where was God in all of this?

Ted felt like he was being eaten alive with envy. He could not begin to be genuinely happy for his friend because his own concerns got in the way. It was one of his worst moments. As he realized that, an image of Jesus suddenly came to his mind and he was stunned by the contrast. In Christ's worst moments, what had he been like? He had cared about the people around him. Love controlled him.

There was something about the stark contrast in Ted's response and the one he saw in Jesus that moved him to a profound sense of worship and awe. A small phrase spoken by the father to the disgruntled prodigal son came to his mind. "I have always loved you and all that I have is yours," the father had said.[1] Ted realized that God was dealing differently in his life than in his friend's, but no less graciously.

So it is that in facing disappointment, there is much that shifts inside us, much that changes about the way we view our faith and ourselves.

AN HONEST HEART

What is necessary in order to really move into the kind of open-ended trust that marks genuine spiritual growth? Perhaps, to begin with, that transition requires an honest heart most of all, a response more difficult than it sounds. Facing disappointment with God often means sorting through a tangled knot of emotions—anger, grief, rebellion, bewilderment. Such messy scenes may be permissible with a friend or spouse or even one of our children. But God? For him, we tend to make ourselves more presentable, to stay dressed in our Sunday best. It's easier to paste a smile on our face and pretend. To be honest with God on this level of disappointment seems a gutsy proposition.

When the miscarriage of a dream seems hopelessly intertwined with your faith, when in some crazy way it was *God* that didn't live up to your expectations, then the most natural inclination is simply to turn away. That kind of backward motion can be accomplished in a variety of ways, both subtle and blatant. Some people escape into an affair, or pursue a sport or graduate school or a new business idea with renewed vigor. But more often, we choose quieter means of giving up, much like letting the air leak slowly out of your tires until you are left sitting motionless. The most effective means of turning away, however, is to never really admit that you were even disappointed.

After Susan's divorce and her return home with two small children in tow, she kept herself distracted with the business of starting life over. There was plenty to keep her occupied. She noticed, from time to time, how rarely she prayed, and that when she did, it was only superficially. Her Bible was tucked away in a bedroom drawer she did not open for months. None of this was by design exactly. It just kind of happened that way.

Sudden outbursts of frustration with her kids seemed to come out of nowhere and she found them frightening. She had a strong urge to slam the door on her boss every time she walked out of his office. Cynical thoughts played around the edge of her mind, but for the most part, she managed to keep them to herself.

It was a friend's offhand remark that got her attention. She had just spent an hour listening to Susan complain about her tight finances. As she reached for the restaurant bill, she remarked, "You sound like a pretty angry woman."

Susan began to think about that. Could it be anger that hid behind her cool front? Maybe she was angry—and hurt and disappointed as well.

That Jim was the focal point of that anger and pain was obvious to Susan. His face was the clearest one in her mind. She was down on herself, too. What was hard for Susan to face was her anger with God. She felt as though she had been betrayed by him, even though she knew her decision to marry Jim was her own choice.

There is at least one example in the Bible of someone whose spiritual struggle centers around the feeling of betrayal. Jeremiah, who was drafted by God into a post as a prophet in Judah, knew that the task of being God's spokesman to a rebellious nation was no dream job. He knew he would encounter the wrath of kings and the deaf ear of his countrymen. But when a fellow priest named Pashhur had Jeremiah beaten and put in stocks, Jeremiah sank to an all-time low. He did not seem to be prepared for opposition that came from another "servant of God."

At this point, Jeremiah's story stops and we are given audience to a profoundly personal prayer, revealing a man struggling with the unexpected circumstances God allowed in his life. "O Lord," Jeremiah says, "Thou hast deceived me and I was deceived; Thou has overcome me and prevailed."[2] Jeremiah simply began to pray about his confusion. He admitted the worst of it. "I feel betrayed, let down, angry and overcome," he says. On one level, he felt deceived by God and on another, he knew he had deceived himself. He made no attempt to sort it all out— he simply brought the whole tangled mess to the Lord. He was counting on the strength of one who could bear the weight of such honesty.

When Susan got the courage to bring an honest heart to God, when she allowed herself to admit the anger and disappointment she felt, she found herself surprised. "It was as though God had been waiting all that time for me to invite him into the middle of all of that," she says. "It was like he stepped out from behind a curtain. After months and months of feeling almost no connection with him at all, I was bowled over by the immediacy of his presence."

Slowly, mysteriously, the ability to forgive Jim, other Christians, even God, began to take shape. "I've come to think," Susan says now, "that forgiveness in places where there's been a lot of hurt is really something supernatural, a gift as well as a choice."

There is tremendous freedom when we gather the courage to get honest, when we stop running and hiding and pretending. We come emptyhanded to the Lord, carrying nothing but an open heart, and God takes that honesty and transforms it into saving grace.

DISAPPOINTMENT: AN UNLIKELY ROUTE TO FAITH

Getting honest with God was the first step for Susan, a new chapter in a slow process of rebuilding her life. She began to realize that for years she had owned a kind of "lazy man's faith," where she simply accepted whatever someone told her. She never really took it out and examined it for herself.

When she began to do that, for a while, everything was up for question. "I started over from scratch," she says. "The most I could say at some points was that there is a God and he sent Jesus to die for my sins. Slowly, I've added more back, and what I have now is mine, really mine."

Susan speaks with the quiet sort of confidence of someone who has experienced a deep sense of spiritual renewal, a reconversion. What she believes and the way she feels are more of an integrated whole. There is freedom to question. "I wouldn't wish this kind of pain on anyone," she says, "but in many ways the best thing that ever happened to me was that it all fell apart."

Who would ever guess that faith itself would be one of those things you have to lose, in some ways, in order to find, that it's possible to be less sure of the answers and more certain of God, or that when you finally let go of the determination to make God conform in safe, predictable ways, you receive something better in its place?

I am convinced that real faith is alien to human nature. It's not part of the air I breathe. What for years I've passed off as faith has been little more than an effort to take what I understood about God and shape that knowledge into something I could get my hands around. Like the Constitution of the United States, faith was a set of propositions to be analyzed, explained, and defended with your blood.

I suspect that much of what I have formerly called faith is little better than having invited God into the parlor of my life while I went to check his references. I was not sure that I could risk giving him the full run of the place. Sometimes I have felt frustrated with his apparent absence, wondering why he so seldom seemed present in a more immediate way. And at other times I have wanted him to go away and leave me be, like a UPS dispatcher who kept bringing packages to my door I did not order.

What I see in Susan's life, though, and what I sense God is moving me toward, is something qualitatively different. It is a faith that looks more like an open hand than a clenched fist—a faith that is wider and freer and more at ease with uncertainty.

This kind of open-ended trust always seems to come unexpectedly. Only after you've been disillusioned with what seemed like faith, only after some stinging disappointment causes your box to collapse. The utter paradox is that this kind of trust begins in those unlikely moments when there is no experiential reason to believe. Only then is there room for real faith to take root. It is born in the fearlessness that comes when you've already lost a good portion of what you were so afraid of losing in the first place. It sprouts at a point of contradiction.

There are three basic options in our response to life and faith, explains Gerald May in his book, *Addiction and Grace.* The first is that we ignore God's call on our lives and turn our desires and energies elsewhere. That is simple enough. Secondly, we can fashion a spiritual system that will enable us to feel a measure of power and control rather than *dependence.* In an absurd way, we use what we know about God to try to keep him contained.

Or we may finally choose what May calls the contemplative option, which he says signals the beginning of "an intentional spiritual life." The contemplative option is a willingness "to face life in a truly undefended and open-eyed way . . . [It] is a simple courageous attempt to bear as much as one can of reality just as it is."[3] Not pretending, not running away, but facing life head-on.

The movement toward genuine faith is marked by choosing to trust God even when we know that the outcome may be something far different than we had ever imagined. We let go of some of our preconceived notions of how things ought to be. If life is a river, we jump right out into the middle of the stream and let it take us where it will. Our trust is open-ended.

This kind of faith is new to me. I hardly know how to make my way around in it yet. Spiritual prescriptions and techniques on how to live the Christian life—I have a whole repertoire of those. But I am just now moving beyond the simple answers into a place where I can enjoy a relationship with a Person, sometimes elliptical, full of ebb and flow, desert and garden. I am learning to let the dissonance feed my new-found trust.

Maybe we who speak of "receiving Christ" do ourselves an injustice by connecting that phrase purely with the act of becoming a Christian. In actuality, we receive him not only once, but many, many times over our lives. That's why disappointment with God can be such an effective catalyst for faith, a ripening of trust that is born on his terms. Sometimes it feels as fresh as conversion. When this begins to happen, we once again encounter the hidden wealth in a disappointed dream.

Growing up spiritually means a progression through a series of "ifs." We begin by wondering "what-if": What if this happens or that happens? Can I make it? Can I find a way to keep my fears from taking over? Or we dabble in a lot of "if-onlys": If only I had a better job or house or marriage, then my life would be set. I would be happy.

But real faith means moving to another kind of "if" entirely. *Even if.* Even if my marriage fails or the roof over my head falls—no matter what—you can count me in. I'm here for the long haul because I realize there is no one else to turn to, and no where else I'd rather be.

CHAPTER 12

Saving The World

What Happened When We Didn't

Under those coats and ties, my genera-
tion is as activistic and idealistic as it
ever was. They're just waiting to redis-
cover the sense of mission they once
had.

Jack Simms, 39

---◆---

On a recent summer trip overseas with my husband, I happened on an unusual opportunity. I was invited to join fifteen others on an old fishing boat leaving for a snorkeling expedition off the coast of Malaysia in the South China Sea. They had room for one more passenger. I packed my gear quickly and took off, ready for an adventure.

Along about the second afternoon, while sitting on the deck being warmed by a cup of hot tea, I realized we must be close to the end of the world. The natives on the tiny island of Au, the place we'd chosen to drop anchor, had lived and mated and died on this two mile stretch of land in the Pacific for generations. They had gotten along quite well without flush toilets, telephones, or dental floss. I was about as far removed from civilization as one can get.

Just as I got to the end of my tea and settled back in the sun ready to listen to the quiet, I began to hear a faint strain of music. Somebody around here had a radio.

Not wanting to miss a thing, I waited to catch the sound of something authentic and oriental—even the primitive rhythms of some tribe in Borneo. But no, this music sounded vaguely familiar. I strained to catch a few of the words. Here, in the middle of nowhere, what was I listening to—again? "Stop—in the name of love, before you break my heart . . ." Here on an island in the South China Sea, with not an English-speaking soul around, I was listening to Diana Ross and The Supremes. I could hardly believe my ears. Boomer music, as my kids say.

I had to smile. Our generation has not moved the world the way we thought we would. But we've done a good job of serenading it.

Every generation, I suppose, has its lost ideals—the dreams and myths that gave it momentum and identity. Those of us who fed on the great expectations and big dreams that accompanied our youth were caught in an interesting paradox.

Due to the sheer size of our numbers, we assumed a place right near the center of everyone's attention. Feeling special was normal. But the size of our generation also meant something more than feeling special. It meant obscurity. The individual had to shine and shine brightly, so as not to be lost in the crowd. Out of that paradox was born a tremendous *longing for significance.*

The thought that one might just muddle through life and leave behind nothing much to show for it was totally unappealing. We wanted the world to be different for our having been here. "I want to make my life count," was our rallying cry.

Simply put, we wanted to change the world.

I blush now to write those words, half-embarrassed twenty years later that I succumbed to the grandiosity of such idealism. Yet as much as I recognize the naivete in thinking we could do what other generations tried hard and failed to accomplish—that we could correct problems centuries old *now*—that longing to make a difference still runs deep. Little vestiges of wanting to change the world filter yet through my everyday experience.

Like the weight of personal responsibility I feel to *do* something when I drive by the local juvenile prison and see a sea of fatherless boys from Raleigh's inner city on the basketball court out back.

Or in Susan's life, the way she looks for a way to derive meaning out of a failed marriage—something she can share with someone else in the same struggle.

Like Grant in his steady pursuit of ways to integrate psychology and theology so that Christianity speaks in relevant language to real needs.

Even Ted, who in the middle of shuffling around figures and flowers all day, tries to influence the people who work for him for Christ. These are some of the ways in which old dreams persist in each of our lives, taking different and usually more specific shapes now than they used to.

BIG DREAMS, BIG DISAPPOINTMENTS

Our generation grew up looking upon a need as an opportunity—an opportunity with our name on it. War, poverty, prejudice, we looked out of a world that needed saving, and still does. For those of us who were in Sunday school twenty-five years ago—or some version thereof—our solution to the world's problems took on a spiritual shape. The Great Commission, Christ's departing words to take the gospel to the ends of the earth, provided a way to change the heart of man and consequently, the problems of the world. Here was a measurable dream, small increments that added up to a large whole. One person was the key to many more. Between the power of the gospel and a steady supply of adrenalin and eager faces, reaching the world for Christ seemed like a do-able proposition.

Here was also a tangible means of making your life count, a way to rise out of anonymous obscurity. Being a small part of a big movement was special. I felt, personally, as though I had been let in on a great secret. What could be more exciting than seeing the gospel take hold in another person's life, especially if that person was just one in a chain of future manys? I dismissed things like engagement rings or choosing a major as mere trivialities by comparison. Against a backdrop of reaching the world for Christ, it is easy to understand why our longing for significance was wedded to the concept of size. Here was a dream on the largest scale possible.

The idea of changing the world in your generation calls for big strategies, large armies of man-power, money, and other effective tools. A kind of drivenness takes over and the Great Commission becomes the Great Task to be performed. A giant gospel machine. In striving toward such a huge goal, it becomes hard to tell whether the individual is the end or the means to the end, or a confusing mix of both.

Here is where the hope of making a difference, spiritually packaged on such a large scale, easily derails; where it becomes as much burden as opportunity; where it gets calcified in global projections. For if one person shares the gospel with ten others, there are twenty more standing right behind them who also need to hear. There is no end in sight. No matter what you do, the world never seems much less in need of saving.

Dreams that are so big, so inherently unreachable, tend to dwarf the individual efforts needed to fulfill them. Big is not just better—big is all that really matters. Those kinds of dreams have a disturbing tendency to backfire, for unless you can come up with a way to make sense of your small part, you are destined to be disappointed. When the big dream proves undoable, you are left asking if anyone else missed the train besides you. You are wondering—still wondering—how on earth to make your life count for something significant.

Perhaps the tale of our generation, as contrasted with our parents', is told in the difference between the soldier of World War II and the one in Vietnam. Our fathers returned from Europe and Asia on top of the world, having liberated whole countries from oppressive dictators and receiving the applauses and embraces of fellow Americans for a job well done. Men and women in our generation came back from Vietnam having made the same sacrifice in an unwinnable, highly unpopular war. They received no fanfare, no pats on the back. They got jeers instead of cheers, a homeland with its back turned rather than arms outstretched. Sacrifice lost some of its nobility. It can be terribly costly, and we learned that sometimes, it turns out much differently than you expected.

Vietnam, which was followed closely by the national embarrassment of Watergate and a presidential resignation, significantly lowered our sights as a generation. All that immense effort had changed very little. The wheels of power seemed sure to grind steadily onward and the world no longer appeared as reachable for Christ. So we set out to discover smaller dreams, and the less dramatic, individualized roles we could play in effecting change.

NEW FORMS TO OLD DREAMS

Bittersweet. That's the word sometimes used to describe that era of grand, noble dreams. In spite of the fact that we brought about an earlier end to Vietnam, we still lost the war. Maybe the problem of racial inequality got more of the attention it deserved, but basically, the problems remained. The world still needs as much saving. We never quite got there, though we are different people, better people for all the desire.

Where did all that hunger for meaning and purpose and impact go? What did we do with the disappointment that comes from downscaling such big dreams?

For a long time, it appeared that our generation turned in to itself and turned sour on outside concerns. We stopped trying so hard to save the world. But media-worn caricatures of our generation as navel-gazing couch potatoes are short-sighted. Our vision may have narrowed and the scope of our concern become more localized, but many of our longings for impact are still very much intact.

They are not dead, but latent—and reemerging with a variety of different shapes and characteristics.

Low-Key Change Agents

When it became harder to make big waves, we developed finer skills in making the smaller ones more effective. We went to work inside the very structures we had challenged. Many of the values that marked our earlier ideals are still very much present, flavoring our approach and outlook on the things we touch.

Inside the church, where the Pepsi generation and the Harry Truman generation sit in the same pew, change is often slow. Like the ninety-five-year-old lady who said the thing she liked best about her church was that nothing had changed since she was eight years old, ideas about what the church is and what the church should be about are deeply rooted. As the postwar generation has matured and begun to take on positions of leadership, though, the influence of their values—vestiges of earlier dreams—can be felt.

One particular emphasis remains in the necessity of owning your own contribution. Personal responsibility is key. We have preferred a stake in the action. Let me *do* something about a problem rather than just wade through theological debate and endless speculation.

"I'm not content with relegating ministry to the professional," says a man who owns a string of nursing homes in the Northeast. He feels his job overseeing care for the elderly is as much ministry as it is business. It is not a secondary calling. Half of his clientele is Jewish and the ethical issues that surround death and dying are everyday fare for him. This is the arena in which he has chosen to live out spiritual realities. "The church doesn't exist to make me feel good," he believes. "I'm being fed so that I can do something out there where it counts." This man sees himself as a change agent in a highly specialized setting.

Another way in which the presence of this generation is being felt in the church is in the current emphasis on the relational dimension to the gospel. Our longing for significant relationships has produced an explosion in the use of small groups as opportunities for individuals to connect with the support of other individuals, and learn from them. We have wanted models we could learn from, examples of truth fleshed out. Aside from all the verbiage, is there a real person with honest struggles behind the message? The ring of authenticity is one we listen closely for. It's a value that crops up over and over again.

One middle-aged seminary professor on the West Coast admits that he is emerging from a period where he had grown cynical about Christianity in this culture. "I finally realized," he says, "that I was disillusioned with Christianity *as it appears in mass form.* It's entirely too predictable. It's the public image of organized Christianity that discourages me." What has kept him moving forward has been what he calls "pockets of authentic Christianity." He can sight particular individuals whose lives testify to something that is real and genuine. Seeing people in small groups who are deeply committed to each other continues to persuade him that real spirituality exists in the context of community.

Hidden under the low-key change agentry to which our big dreams evolved, there is still the longing to challenge the norm. Beneath the coats and ties, a radical edge lingers. We tend to be uncomfortable with the status quo, willing to rock the boat when needed.

"At the funniest times I realize that I'm still a refugee of the '60s," explains the chaplain of Duke University, a southern citadel of tradition. The students who come to his office these days are timid, insecure with even the mildest forms of dissent, afraid that a letter urging the board toward divestiture may be too bold. He is in a strange position. He is the establishment now. Yet he finds himself inwardly aghast, wanting to say "You weenies! Where's your spine?" His wife reminds him when he speaks in chapel that, after all, this is Duke. Perhaps he's being a bit too outspoken, too undignified.

"I take that as a compliment," he says. To him, conflict is just part of the change process, the part that tells him "something's happening."

Patience in the Process

One of the changes for the better in our matured approach to the ideals of our youth is that somewhere in the process, we seem to have acquired a bit of patience. This is another characteristic of the new approach we've given to old dreams.

Nothing much happens quickly—only laxatives work overnight—and slowly but surely, our demand to see immediate results has mellowed. Instead of a sole focus on the desired outcome, there is an appreciation for the process of getting there. Not just the arrival, but also the journey takes on significance.

Somewhere in the back of Ted's mind, part of his reason for going into business for himself was the hope of having an impact on the people who worked for him. He saw his business as a platform. Out of his success, his employees would just come to him in search of his spiritual secret, or so he thought.

His story didn't work out that way. He found his failures and set-backs to be humbling, and for a short while, he was tempted to just distance himself from his employees. What kind of testimony did he have, anyway? What could he tell them? His life was no great advertisement for a simply-trust-God kind of faith.

Instinctively, though, Ted knew he couldn't live that way. He chose not to hide what was really happening. "I let them share in some of the struggle, offer advice, feel some of the frustration with me. We started to tackle this thing together," Ted explains. He chose to set up a profit-sharing plan during a time when the natural tendency would have been to hang on to every dime.

For a period of two years, Ted met with two other businessmen one morning a week. There in the back of his store, before the day started, they would spend some time in Bible study, encouraging each other. Ted said little about it. He needed the group for his own sanity.

One day, right in the middle of a staff meeting, one of his employees spoke up and challenged Ted. "How come you get with these other men to study the Bible, and you've never offered anything like that to us?" he said. Ted didn't know what to make of this. The guys who worked for him were more likely to frequent a happy hour than a Bible study. He never even thought of making such a suggestion. One by one they all chimed in. In much the same way they deliberated over a new marketing plan, they chose a day to begin.

Recently, as Ted was distributing fliers for a design show to all the salesmen, he happened to notice that on each desk, right in the middle of the invoices and brochures, there sat a Living Bible. The sight was a metaphor. "The people who work for us are not the kind who come to Christ and the next day they've cleaned up their act. These people have lived it all," he says. To see this level of spiritual openness among them has gone a long way to making the last five years worth the haul.

Slowly, by a strange, circuitous route, Ted has found himself in the middle of the kind of ministry he wanted —natural and unforced. The best part, he says, is that this wasn't something he orchestrated or sweated blood to make happen. It grew out of the humility of failure and unblanching honesty. It grew out of patience.

There is something redeeming about having to go the long way around sometimes. You get the benefit of hindsight. You get to see all the seemingly small things that added up to more than you would have thought. You come away with the sense that much of what is truly significant rarely *feels* that way at the time.

Joy in the Genuine

We didn't change the world. We didn't even come remotely close. What has changed, in fact, has been the shape of our original longings.

It's hard to reach the world with a two-year-old clinging to your skirt. You can't rewrite nuclear policy and still get your marketing plan finished by Friday. The course of western civilization probably won't be terribly altered by your research dissertation on Carl Jung. Those big dreams get broken up into smaller pieces, the way phrases are broken by hyphens and commas in a runaway sentence.

The great numbers and longitudinal projections have evolved into something that looks more relational and fluid, more like concentric circles than geometric lines and pyramids. We seem to have traded some of our affinity for the large and showy for a deeper experience of the genuine. I asked a woman recently why she continued, week after week, to hold quiet recovery groups for women who had had abortions. Her answer, I felt, spoke for many people making little contributions in soup kitchens and homeless shelters, or among drug–addicted teenagers and declining old ladies. "I found that in this group I was perched right on the ledge of watching the deepest truths of the gospel take root in one of the most hidden of all secrets—that of allowing the life of your own child to be taken," she said. In other words, she was able to participate in the changed lives of a few individuals, and that was both enough and a lot. What happens beyond that point, only God knows.

On the same summer trip overseas, I happened to squeeze in two totally different experiences on the same day. The contrast between them I recognize to be a parable of sorts.

In Singapore I went out shopping for the day and found myself on Orchard Road. I had only vaguely heard of Orchard Road, but in short order I realized I was in a shopper's paradise. Gucci and Christian Dior and Rolex, silks, laces, jewelry and electronics—a good sampling of everything made in the world was for sale here. The dazzle, the spectacle before me pumped up all my adrenalin, and before too many hours had passed, I had spent my little wad. The whole experience was exhilarating. Yet I came home feeling bone tired and about as plastic as my charge card, wondering what on earth that was all about.

That same evening Stacy and I met with a group of Indian couples who had asked us to share something of what we were learning about marriage in midlife. Though we had never met them, though their culture, accent and dress, and the color of their skin were all vastly different from our own, I was instantly aware of feeling right at home. There was an immediacy of connection with them, a warmth and ease in their presence that one could only explain as the Lord. Yet it was a simple evening. Nothing extraordinary took place. We shared back and forth about the struggles and frustrations, the unexpected pleasures of having lived with the same person for fifteen years or so. The delight I found was the simple thrill of taking part in someone else's life —of being touched by their involvement in mine.

I realized later that I had spent too many years looking for the Orchard Roads of the Christian life. My craving for the momentous had almost spoiled me for being able to appreciate the joy in the ordinary. My attachment to some big dream had blinded me to those little, unpredictable, incandescent moments with people, when what is experienced is nothing less than the life of God in us and between us.

I'm not sure when it finally dawned on me that if you took everything my life was about, it still wouldn't add up to all that much. Or that all my efforts would never bring me a permanent fix of significance and meaning. Or that if I continued to measure the worth of my life by the size of what it accomplished, I would be in trouble. I'm only glad it did.

I still long to see the world change. But I've grown much more content with my small contribution. The guilt of not doing it all rests lighter on my shoulders. Though I have the same heart, I have narrowed my field. Or as Madeline L'Engle says beautifully in one of her poems:

> To grow up
> is to find
> the small part you are playing
> in this extraordinary drama
> written by
> Somebody else.[1]

CHAPTER 13

Fresh Starts
Embracing a Realistic Hope

What I know now, but I didn't know then, is that there are no secrets or short cuts to growing up.

Cheryl Merser, 39

———————————◆———————————

Just inside the entrance of a retreat center in the valley of Virginia, four similar paintings hang together as a group. The subject matter is simple. In each painting there is a boat with a sole occupant heading down a river toward the lights of a city in the distance. It is the progression that tells the story.

The artist intends to let you see the classic passages of life through visual metaphor. In the first painting, a baby sleeps in the boat as the smooth current carries the boat gently along. The second picture depicts a rugged young man standing in the rear of the boat, the steering wheel firmly within his grip and his eyes fixed on the bright lights of a distant city. He is strong and capable and in control, heading resolutely toward his dreams.

The third painting tells another story. The water churns like rapids in a deep river gorge, spraying fine mists over the side of the boat. A low-lying fog obscures the lights of that once-bright city, and the captain of this ship is no longer young and no longer standing. His hands are nowhere near the steering wheel. He's on his knees in the back of the boat hanging on for dear life, a look of distress on his face.

The last picture is the best of all. An old man, slightly worn around the edges, sits peacefully in the boat with his hand lightly resting on the wheel. Neither the lines of resignation nor striving crease his cheeks. He is at ease. The years have taught him how to relax and trust the boat and the current to carry him along.

These paintings hold a viewer's attention because they give an overview of a journey we are all taking. These are four distinct stages in life, four passages common to anyone's normal life span. If you identify with the man in the third painting in this series—not old but no longer young—there is something especially comforting about recognizing the flux and confusion, the panic and disappointment for the common responses that they are.

For our generation, those responses are almost predictable, given our backgrounds. For us who count ourselves among the generation born to parents elated by the victory of World War II, our transition—from idealistic youth seeking our own bright vistas, to sobered, middle-aged adults often overwhelmed with life—has been much harder. We have known an even rougher-than-normal passage.

If you sense yourself somewhere in this process of negotiating your way through the middle of life, there is some encouraging news. Most transitions, especially midlife, follow three fairly predictable stages.[1] The first is probably the hardest. Some inner restlessness begins to call for change, but it's not clear what kind or how much. It may feel as though you've outgrown the place you're in; a particular role or task no longer fits you.

When you sense yourself in this first phase of disenchantment, what you need most is some time to reassess, to sort out, to look for what may be missing. Ironically, what has aided you up to this point—your self-image, style of relating, approach to a task—may hinder you from the kind of growth called for now. What got you this far may not take you where you want to go. Ted, for instance, spent the first half of his life as a lone ranger, used to battling against the odds by sheer force of individual determination. His business difficulties forced him to take a mental "time out." There he realized he needed a more participatory approach to work. He needed to learn how to call out someone else's talents.

The second stage in such a passage is called the neutral zone. This is a fallow period, sometimes painful, more often just flat and shapeless. The great tendency is to rush out and try a quick fix or to push yourself through to the next phase. But it is the person who gives himself time and space who experiences real renewal. To just push down the inner issues and go on when those issues need to surface is to find they come up again later—with added wallop. Those who take the time to regroup now come out stronger in the end.

Eventually, the neutral zone gives way to a new beginning. Your energy and zest returns; some new venture or way of relating beckons and you are able to move forward. "The lesson of all such experience is that when we are ready to make a beginning, we will shortly find an opportunity."[2]

Part of growing up, in the fuller sense of the word, is learning how to make sense of your own journey. It means recognizing your expectations and digesting your disappointments. It is coming to terms with life as it is as well as how it ought to be. It is letting go and moving on with hope, not resignation.

RIDING LOOSER IN THE SADDLE

For many people, the decade between ages thirty-five and forty-five is marked by mini-losses, by a sense of dissatisfaction, by the struggle to turn dreams into reality. Somewhere along the way it's easy to lose sight of the opportunity we're being offered. There are gains as well as losses. Part of the hidden wealth in disappointed dreams is that we are offered the chance to lay hold of a different approach to life.

Susan feels that experiencing a failed marriage, while she would never have wanted that, has nevertheless built a resilience and depth in her life that wasn't there before. She has not only survived divorce, she has grown through the pain. "It's one thing to believe in yourself at twenty," she says. "But when you've survived a broken world experience and even overcome in places, then you start to believe there's something of serious substance there."

Susan's divorce has also changed her relationships for the better. "I feel less need for a fantasy person, less need to idealize other people," she explains. She can recognize their gifts and abilities, their special competencies, but their mixed motivations and internal struggles are no longer such a mystery to her. In her relationship with God, she experiences a reciprocity that wasn't there before. There's freedom to interact, a confidence that if she gives something time, the truth will rise to the surface.

Susan is the first to admit that she lives in the daily reminders of unfulfilled longings. There are gaps in her girls' experience that leave her with the same old ache. No matter how hard she tries, she can't be both father and mother. Between her children's needs and her own, she is often tired and worn out, feeling at times as though her greatest parenting accomplishment is just, as she says, that she "showed up." Yet she feels the quiet satisfaction of living out her faith in circumstances that fall short of anyone's ideal.

Once you've made it through some significant disappointments, new ones lose a little of their sting. You can be disappointed but not devastated, and there is a vast difference between those two. The person who is disappointed prepares to weather the crisis; the one who is devastated severely doubts that he can. Part of the hidden gift to the person who has faced crisis and survived is that he rides looser in the saddle from that point forward. He is not wasting bundles of energy braced and tense, working overtime to keep his carefully constructed dreams from crashing about his feet. His hands are no longer gripped, white-knuckled around the steering wheel.

FREER OF ILLUSIONS

What the disenchantment of our dreams also does for us is to shake us free from many of our illusions about life. We are *dis-illusioned,* and while that word has a negative connotation, the process is a decidedly positive thing. It's a key ingredient, a necessary part of what it means to embrace reality.

Part of the baggage of youth is the half-formed idea that your real life will begin at the next major juncture in the road. Just around the corner. Somewhere out there, a bright tomorrow holds the feeling of completion that eludes you today. When you are single and twenty-five, marriage is the answer to what ails you. Or it's a good job. Then you have a few children. You buy a house and settle down. But each new step fails to bring you any closer, really, to the end of the rainbow. You can't seem to reach the place where all the jagged pieces of life fit into a nice tight whole.

Growing up is about facing that small, incessant ache in your own soul and realizing it's never going to go away in this life. It wasn't meant to.

For Grant, moving out into the suburbs where he could establish his own practice was the event he'd been holding out for. But when this bright future tomorrow actually became today and the aura faded, he discovered he was pretty much the same guy with a new set of problems. "There wasn't any more real peace and sanity here than there had been in the city," he says. "I wasn't living on easy street."

The illusion he was forced to let go of was what he calls the idea of "the perfect life." There was no fixed set of variables he could get all lined up at the same time that would baptize his life with "happiness." And with that deep realization, he found unexpected freedom. "I've seen what a joke it is to think I could finally come upon the key to a perfect life," he says. "Once I let go of that illusion, I find I'm enjoying life in the present in a new way—my kids, my marriage, my patients, me." He feels able to live in the confusion and ambiguity of it all without his old franticness, his perfectionistic tendencies to Do It Right.

It's not as though he has given up on his dreams. He continues to piece together, bit by bit, what he thinks of as a kind of "liberation theology of the soul." He feels the church is on the verge of a second reformation, a new attempt to allow Christianity to speak to the real needs of modern man. He'd like to be there with a model, a blending of psychology and theology, that will work. But at this point, he is not living in suspended animation until his dreams materialize.

Grant's illusion of "the perfect life" is a common myth that any of us can fall for. It is just one of many false hopes we let go of in order to grow.

EMBRACING LIFE

In Madeline L'Engle's trilogy of books that form her autobiography, she writes about her maternal grandmother, Mado, a southern lady who lost her husband at a young age and lived through years of poverty in the Reconstruction days of the South. She describes Mado as an old woman with that "peculiar quality of aliveness" that comes to people who have already done a lot of their dying.[3] It intrigues me that vibrancy of life should be connected to loss and dying dreams. The two would appear contradictory. But there is a freedom found in letting go, in dying to some of our false hopes. We begin to realize that we can't control the world—not even our own world. It is a humbling recognition that brings relief.

Here, in the middle of life, is the point where we come to an invisible fork in the road. We can either try to reduce the scope of our world to a size that *appears* controllable, or we can take a wide and risky, energizing step. We can refuse the temptation to batton down the hatch and instead, open ourselves to receive the people and experiences that come our way. We can trade certainty for adventure, and in the process begin to come alive in a new way. Like Steve Martin in the movie *Parenthood*, we learn to laugh more on the rollercoaster and enjoy the ride.

Accepting life as it is, in some ways, is an even greater feat than realizing your dreams. Says one friend, "In my family we always called this kind of person, a 'maintainer,' and we kind of sneered when we said the word. But I have come to see that acceptance can be a strong, magnificent thing—something that Jesus himself had to do." Making peace with life as it is can be as noble as reaching for the stars, as good as John Wayne taking the West. It's as much a part of life as realizing all your best hopes.

This is how dying dreams can so often give birth to something almost better, to that paradoxical quality of "aliveness" that characterized Madeline L'Engle's grandmother. Embracing life as it is releases you to experience the most of what is actually before you. Mere life can hold fresh joy. Lesser, at times, becomes mysteriously more.

Part of the freedom at this point in life is the potential ability to give to others without strings attached. This is what developmental theorists call generativity.[4] Some of that bundle of energy to prove yourself gets rechanneled into a capacity to mentor others and to bring them along. Many people feel this is the path to replenishment in the middle of life. In the freedom of not having to push ahead, when that do–or–die compulsion subsides, then we are able to invest in others for their sakes. We no longer look at someone else as an extension of ourselves quite so much, or as a means toward our own all–important end.

This is what Ted discovered when his business didn't take off the way he had hoped it would. For a long time, all he saw was the goals he would probably never reach. What stood out to him was his own failure to achieve the kind of success for which he'd hoped. He almost missed the really special things that were happening around him because he was so busy looking for something else.

"I finally got to the point where I could see there was something blossoming around me, and it was people. The pleasure shifted focus. Helping these guys who worked for me feel an ownership in what they were doing, watching them develop, these were the things that seemed to matter—as much as creating a big, successful company had in the past," he says.

More and more, there is a note of sheer gratefulness that comes out in Ted's reflections on the last five years. His children have learned a lot, they've been able to keep their house, his business is making some slow, steady gains, a few of his employees have found Christ. "The goodness of God is what stands out to me these days— that he doesn't want or need anything from us, that he never, never lets us go."

GRATITUDE

I recently read an interview with Sylvester Stallone, the forty-three-year-old Rocky who turns to painting when he is not acting. His life impresses me as one that models so much of the general angst of our generation. Somewhere inside each of his paintings is the picture of a clock. He owns thirty watches and rarely sleeps the night through. It's a waste of time. He sees his strength, his youth, his time quietly slipping past him. He is driven to find that mythical point where all his dreams converge and crystallize and leave him dazzled by their brilliance.

We may not own that many watches, but most of us know what it's like to hear the encroachment of age clicking like a metronome in our ears.

When a person has faced his dreams head-on, though, when he's been forced to reshape a few and let go of others, then the passage of time is not so threatening. He is not looking for some event to give him meaning. It's not later when I get my Ph.D. or build a house or establish a home for unwed mothers. It's life as it's happening now, right under my nose.

This new-found ability to enjoy life as it is leads to a quiet sense of gratitude. And perhaps gratitude is what you least expect to feel after wading through a time of finding new shapes to old dreams. I found personally that it snuck up on me from behind when I least suspected. It caught me quite off guard.

I first noticed that gratitude in the form of lightness. It's amazing how your dreams can become such burdens. To be more relieved of the need to do something remarkable means freedom. When your life doesn't always have to be validated by some external source, you can begin to enjoy so much more. It's striking to me how much simple pleasure there is in relationships when your children and your spouse are not feeling the unspoken pressure to compensate for your unrealized expectations of life.

"Some luck lies in not getting what you thought you wanted," wrote Garrison Keillor, "but getting what you have which once you have it you may be smart enough to see is what you would have wanted all along, had you known."[5] You no longer have to force your life into such a prearranged shape to be happy. You are less afraid to lose, less encumbered, lighter.

What makes that feeling of gratefulness even more unexpected is all the anger and frustration, the sense of loss which preceded it. We would so prefer to go around—not through—that kind of emotional territory, though perhaps it is more necessary than we realize.

This past fall I helped my parents pack up thirty-five years of life in the same home—a house they built right after the war—so they could move to a smaller place without an acre lawn to mow.

On the last day I took a break and snuck off to sit on the swing that had hung for years beneath a huge old oak tree in the yard. That tree has presided, a silent, towering figure, over all the doings of this one family. Once, after World War II, there had been a young couple who cleared the virgin land around this tree and left it standing alone while their home was built. There had been children who spent long summer nights catching lightning bugs, and later on, wedding receptions beneath its boughs. This was certainly one place where I had formed many of my own great hopes for life.

In the last few years, my children had used its barnacled trunk as a base for their games of Hide and Seek. And now, I realized, other families and other generations of children would grow up and live out their lives right here, under the shade of this old tree. The most obvious thought struck me, all the more forcefully because I had lived on top of it all these years. I was now, and always had been, only a *visitor.*

It was one of those moments when I could stand back and see the bigger picture. I could see what a small place I occupied in the overall scheme of things. There is no room to demand that life go a certain way, that it unfold according to my preconceived notions. The world is not my oyster. I'm not going to be here forever. This experience left me a bit more grateful for the small, special pleasures that come my way.

A REALISTIC HOPE

What happened to the Sunday school class of '66? We said we'd never grow up and we'd never grow old; we'd never trust anyone over 30. And now most of us have long since passed that tender age and are in the midst of giving each other black fortieth birthday parties. Who knows? We may yet grow old.

For our generation, more than any other in this century, the twenty-five years between youth and middle age have been marked by unmet expectations. We found many of our dreams unreachable. Growing up for us has been less about realizing our dreams and more about making our dreams subject to reality.

In one sense, when we tied our faith to our cultural expectations, we succumbed to the illusion that we could experience heaven in the here and now. It is true that one day our dreams and longings will be fulfilled beyond our wildest imaginations. Life is going to happen the way it's supposed to, the way we always wanted it to —someday—*but not now.* Now we plow through time, groping, learning, hurting, struggling, failing, and sometimes succeeding. God can help us and strengthen us, but he never promised to keep us from pain. "Our Father refreshes us with some pleasant inns on the journey, but [he] will not encourage us to mistake them for home," wrote C. S. Lewis.[6] No matter what the song says, heaven is not a place on earth.

Perhaps disappointed dreams are our best opportunities to transfer hope to its rightful place. Heaven is where our biggest dreams belong. Realizing that can help us make it through the here and now without placing a burden on the present it was never meant to bear. That's hope—realistic hope—which may serve to carry us through the rest of the journey.

Notes

Chapter One
An Invitation

1. Landon Jones, *Great Expectations: America and the Baby Boom Generation* (New York: Ballantine Books, 1980), 4.

2. John Dawson, *Taking Our Cities for God* (Lake City: Creation House, 1989), 92. 1968–1972 is generally acknowledged as a crucible of time of spiritual interest and awakening especially among youth.

3. Adapted from *Baby Boom Believers* by Mike Bellah (Wheaton: Tyndale House Publishers, 1989), 14, 15.

Chapter Three
Less Than We Bargained For

1. Dave Barry, *Dave Barry Turns 40* (New York: Crown Publishers, 1990), 2.

2. Cheryl Merser, *Grown-Ups: A Generation in Search of Adulthood* (New York: G.P. Putnam's Sons, 1987), 17.

3. Joan Harvey with Cynthia Katz, *The Imposter Phenomenon* (New York: Simon and Schuster, 1984).

4. Gail Sheehy, *Passages* (New York: Bantam, 1977), 376–412.

5. Paul C. Light, *Baby Boomers* (New York: Norton, 1988), 267.

6. Originally from the essay "The 60's Kids and the Crash" by P. J. O'Rourke in *The American Spectator*, February 1988, 16–17.

Chapter Four
The Children of Promise

1. From Morris Massey's video series, "You Are What You Were When," which is a careful synopsis of generational distinctives.

2. Jones, *Great Expectations*, 283.

3. Lamentations 3:27, *NIV*.

4. Jones, *Great Expectations*, 68.

5. Tom Matthews, "The Sixties Complex," *Newsweek*, September 5, 1988, 18.

6. Quoted from *Time*, February 5, 1965, in Jones' *Great Expectations*, 88.

Chapter Five
Beyond the Formulas

1. The most commonly used series was Campus Crusade's "Ten Basic Steps to Christian Maturity," a helpful series of ten booklets on the basic aspects of the Christian life.

2. I am indebted to Paul Borthwick for this analogy.

3. William Bridges, *Transitions: Making Sense of Life's Changes* (Reading: Addison-Wesley, 1980), 37.

4. Mike Bellah, *Baby Boom Believers* (Wheaton: Tyndale, 1988), 9.

Chapter Six
Rude Awakenings

1. Sue Monk Kidd, *When The Heart Waits* (San Francisco: Harper & Row, 1990), 84.

2. Daniel J. Levinson, *The Seasons of a Man's Life* (New York: Knopf, 1978), 71–126.

3. Theodore White, *In Search of History* (New York: Warner, 1978), 525.

Chapter Seven
Inner Spaces

1. Gerald May, *Addiction and Grace* (San Francisco: Harper and Row, 1988), 102.

2. Quoted in Bridges' *Transitions*, 118.

3. John 1:42.

4. John 1:48.

5. Barry, *Dave Barry*, 17.

6. Judith Viorst, *Necessary Losses* (New York: Ballantine, 1986), 299.

7. Randall Jarrell. Quoted from the *New York Times*, December 11, 1983, in Viorst's *Necessary Losses*.

Chapter Eight
Becoming Real

1. Dr. Larry Crabb, *Inside Out* (Colorado Springs: NavPress, 1988), 116–119.

2. 1 Peter 1:5.

Chapter Nine
Loose Connections

1. Martin Seligman, "Boomer Blues," *Psychology Today*, October 1988, 52.

2. Viorst, *Necessary Losses*, 173.

3. See Dan Riley, *Living Together, Feeling Alone: Healing Your Hidden Loneliness* (New York: Prentice Hall, 1989) for further explanation.

4. Sheehy, *Passages*, 358.

5. Bridges, *Transitions*, 58–70.

6. M. Scott Peck, *The Road Less Traveled* (New York: Simon and Schuster, 1978), 68.

7. Judith Viorst, "What is This Thing Called Love?" *Reader's Digest*, August 1975, 65.

Chapter Ten
Making It

1. Cheryl Russell, *100 Predictions for the Baby Boom* (New York: Plenium, 1987), 46.

2. Gilbert Grim, "Losing and Winning," *Psychology Today,* 52.

3. Merser, *Grown-Ups,* 130.

4. Douglas LaBier, *Modern Madness: The Emotional Fallout of Success* (Reading: Addison-Wesley, 1987), 33.

Chapter Eleven
An Honest Faith

1. See Luke 15:31.

2. Jeremiah 20:7, *NASB.*

3. May, *Addiction and Grace,* 107.

Chapter Twelve
Saving the World

1. Reprinted from "Act III, Scene ii" in *The Weather of the Heart* by Madeleine L'Engle © 1978 by Crosswicks. Used by permission of Harold Shaw Publishers, Wheaton, IL.

Chapter Thirteen
Fresh Starts

1. Bridges, *Transitions,* 28–52.

2. Ibid., 136.

3. Madeleine L'Engle, *The Summer of the Great Grandmother* (San Francisco: Harper and Row, 1974), 180.

4. Levinson, *Seasons,* 29.

5. Garrison Keillor, *Lake Wobegon Days* (New York: Viking Penguin, 1985), 337.

6. C. S. Lewis, *The Problem of Pain* (New York: Macmillan, 1962), 115.

About the Author

Paula Rinehart—through her books, magazine articles, and seminars—has offered life-changing spiritual advice benefiting thousands struggling with their faith, interpersonal relationships, and mid-life crises. Having entered the Christian scene during the sixties herself, she has followed the trail of great expectations and big dreams that have so characterized those in the postwar generation. So she knows first-hand what this generation thinks, feels, welcomes, rejects—why they have experienced a crisis of faith, a deep sense of abandonment, and a load of false guilt, and how they can deal with their struggles.

A former acquisitions editor with NavPress, she is the author or coauthor of four previous books, including the 100,000-copy best-seller *Choices: Finding God's Way in Dating, Sex, Singleness, and Marriage,* which was named Campus Life's Book of the Year in 1984.

Paula and her husband, Stacy, have served on the staff of the Navigators for more than ten years. They make their home in Raleigh, North Carolina.

What People Are Saying About This Book

Occasionally a book comes along that challenges the mind and touches the heart of the reader. You are sure the author is writing to you, personally. Paula Rinehart's *Whatever Happened to the Sunday School Class of '66* captures the longing, anxieties, regrets, and heartbeats of my generation. We wanted a little three letter word—*all*. And many of us have discovered all wasn't enough. Paula points us to what has been missing. She offers a mirror and a road map to help us get back on the journey to wholeness in middle age.

I read it with a hi-liter—so will you. This is one book that *will* change your life!

Harold Ivan Smith
Author of *No Fear of Trying*

I was converted in 1968, graduated from college in 1972, and I'm pastoring a church full of "baby-boomers." Does Paula Rinehart's new book have any relevancy for me? You've got to be kidding!

This is one of the most timely, honest, and helpful books that I have read in the last five years. It is full of the fruit born of painful reflection, hopeful longings, and spiritual integrity. The more I read the more I felt like I was a privileged participant in the pilgrimage of fellow sojourners moving through my own early idealism in the faith toward a more substantive and real experience of the grace of the gospel. Paula, thanks for putting into words what I've been feeling in my heart!

> Scotty Smith
> Senior Pastor, Christ
> Community Church
> Franklin, Tennessee

Whatever Happened to the Sunday School Class of '66 is insightful and illuminating reading. All who seek to authentically perceive the dynamic of today's massive baby-boomer population will find Paula Rinehart's book extremely helpful. Combining personal research with insightful reflections from a wide range of authors, this book enables us to more clearly identify and understand the pilgrimage that so many have traveled in the past three decades. I heartily recommend this outstanding work.

> Dr. Ron Lee Davis
> Author of *Mentoring: The
> Strategy of the Master*

Thank you for the chance to read Paula Rinehart's book on the baby-boom generation. Paula has accurately described our disillusionment when we haven't arrived at where we thought we'd be by now. And hooray for her! She doesn't rub salt in our wounds by finishing with another "ten easy steps to a sure-fire solution." We're weary of promises that didn't come true. Instead, she asks us to join her on the journey toward renewed hope and a fresh run at faith. I finished this book aware that I'm never going to have it all, but what I can have could be wonderful if I give God more freedom to be himself.

I thought I was the only one thrashing about in the throes of disappointment because life and God didn't seem to keep their promises. How comforting to find there are a whole booming generation of us. Paula Rinehart has helped give shape to our questions, and given us reason to hope afresh in the God who answers.

Maureen Rank
Author of *Dealing with the Dad of Your Past*

This is one of the four or five best books I have read in my twenty-six years as a Christian.

Paula shows remarkable ability to explain her generation and to make a compelling case for "the narrow way." She has a message every person needs to hear about authentic Christianity. This book needs to be read by all who know that ultimate meaning can only be found in Christ but are finding a secularized Christianity to be little more than a frustrating deadend. Through the lives revealed on these pages, important light is shed on authentic Christianity and the ways it can change a world without hope. This book shines a penetrating searchlight that none of us can afford to ignore.

James F. Engel
Distinguished Professor of Marketing Research and Strategy, Eastern College, Pennsylvania